Political Leadership and Educational Failure

Political Leadership and Educational Failure

Seymour B. Sarason

Jossey-Bass Publishers • San Francisco

Copyright © 1998 by Jossey-Bass Inc., Publishers, 350 Sansome Street, San Francisco, California 94104.

Copyright acknowledgments are on p. 161.

Substantial discounts on bulk quantities of Jossey-Bass books are available to corporations, professional associations, and other organizations. For details and discount information, contact the special sales department at Jossey-Bass Inc., Publishers (415) 433–1740; Fax (800) 605–2665.

For sales outside the United States, please contact your local Simon & Schuster International Office.

Jossey-Bass Web address: http://www.josseybass.com

Manufactured in the United States of America using Lyons Falls D'Anthology paper, which is a special blend of non-tree fibers and totally chlorine-free wood pulp.

Library of Congress Cataloging-in-Publication Data

Sarason, Seymour B.
    Political leadership and educational failure / Seymour B. Sarason. — 1st ed.
      p.   cm.—(The Jossey-Bass education series)
    Includes bibliographical references (p.).
    ISBN 0-7879-4061-5 (hardcover : alk. paper)
    1. Politics and education—United States. 2. Political leadership—United States.
   3. Education and state—United States. 4. Educational change—United States.
   5. Education—United States—Evaluation. I. Title. II. Series.
   LC89.S27   1998
   379—dc21   97-38547

RST EDITION
Printing 10 9 8 7 6 5 4 3 2 1

The Jossey-Bass Education Series

Contents

To
Elizabeth Meyer Lorentz
Friend, Colleague, Mentor

Preface

This is a book about responsibility and accountability in regard to educational reform. Although that theme is a relevant one for diverse groups in the educational arena, I have, as the title of this book indicates, restricted myself to those in the political arena because they have escaped critical scrutiny. That scrutiny is long overdue, and my hope is that what I have written will motivate others to contribute their thoughts and experience. This book could have been much larger, but I decided that the most practical thing I could do would be to pose and discuss the issues—concrete issues of long standing—only in terms of errors of omission and commission by those in high political office. Some people—certainly those in the political arena—will regard the tone and substance of this book as unwarranted, off the mark, and polemical. Though I grant that I pull no punches, I wish to make it clear that I am not impugning or derogating the intelligence and good intentions of those I criticize. Political leaders have felt justified in directing their criticisms to nonpolitical groups for their failure to change and improve our schools. Some of those criticisms are justified, although almost all of them betray unfamiliarity with our system of education and the culture of schools. So, when political leaders feel justified, as they should, in voicing their criticisms, they provide me with justification for scrutinizing and criticizing their undeniably crucial role, their responsibility and accountability for educational reform. It is not an instance of tit for tat. There is too much at stake to play that game.

One of the themes of this book is that in regard to educational reform, presidents and others in high elective office expose their ignorance of the substance and history of the educational reform movement. A second theme is that they are not motivated to try to learn why past efforts at school change have had no impact; if they were motivated they would not repeat what past political leaders have said and done. The third theme is that these leaders, especially presidents, have the authority, resources, and obligation to determine why the fruits of the reform movement have been so few. When you talk about school change, you are not talking about a circumscribed problem; you are talking about an institution that dynamically interacts with all major facets of society. And I say "dynamically" advisedly, because those interactions are never static; they may be slow, quiet, and unremarkable—but not for long. Since the end of World War II the pace and obtrusiveness of those interactions have increased as never before in our national history and, I predict, if we continue on our present course, the road ahead will become even more bumpy, especially in our urban areas.

Given the discouraging results of the educational reform movement over the past half century, one would expect that political leaders would have given us more than empty generalizations, or exhortations and proclamations, or statements of goals that confuse wish fulfillment with reality, or expectations that are as misleading as they are substantively unfounded. But, I found myself asking (about ten years ago), why is it that I expected so little from presidents and others in high elective offices? Why do we elect them to these positions of responsibility? When they are confronted with problems of health care, they seek both to appear and to be knowledgeable; we may not agree with them but we will not say they are abysmally ignorant of all the important issues and their complex interactions. When they are confronted with problems of environmental pollution and they have to act, they engage in a learning process; they cannot afford to remain rank amateurs. But when it comes to the inadequacies of our schools, the seriousness of which they say they know, the threat to the social fabric they say they fear, they say absolutely nothing to suggest they know whereof they speak.

I do not call for these political leaders to become sophisticated educators, but I do assert that if they had the desire to learn more about the issues, if they began to ask the obvious questions, they would be fulfilling the major obligation of their office: to inform, to place that information in a moral-psychological tradition, to begin to see (and to help others see) the options and problems we will confront. Why has the expenditure of scores of billions of dollars had such disappointing consequences? Why does an apparently successful educational innovation not spread to other schools within the same district, and often not even to other class-rooms in that school? What have we learned about the features of contexts of productive and unproductive learning? Why is it that as students go from elementary to middle to high school they become increasingly bored with and disengaged from school learning? What do we know about the adequacy of the hundreds of programs that prepare educators for a career?

Is it expecting too much of a political leader for him or her to ask these and other relatively concrete questions, that is, to appoint commissions to deal with these questions and then for the leader to ensure that the answers—about which there will not be unanimity—get and remain on the societal agenda? For example, why is it that no president has seen fit to appoint a group of knowledgeable people to tell him and the country what are the most important issues in the development of better preparatory programs for educators? Do you have to be a savant, a sage, a deep thinker to suggest that if schools are far from what we want them to be, maybe we ought to look at how educators are selected, trained, credentialed? That question was addressed in 1996 by a nongovernmental group of which Linda Darling-Hammond was executive director. It is a report as disturbing as it is overdue. I predict that the report will have very limited circulation and then only in a special circle. From the standpoint of the general public, the report does not exist. And that is my point: it is a difference that would have made a world of difference if such an exemplary report had been commissioned and promoted by a president who, being able to read English, could not ignore the concrete answers to the concrete questions the report contains. From one standpoint the report is bad news: there is a lot wrong with preparatory programs for educators. From another standpoint the news is good: the bad news has been swept from under the rug, discussion can now begin, respect will be paid to the public's right to know. Unfortunately, the bad and the good news will, for all practical purposes, not be news at all, even though the report speaks to issues that go far beyond the encapsulated classroom in the encapsulated school. Contrast that realistic scenario with the manner in which the report of President Reagan's commission—the title of the report was *A Nation at Risk* (1983)—was promoted, Madison Avenue style, on the front page of newspapers as well as on the evening news hour on TV. That report was a marvel of empty rhetoric; it asked no questions and it gave no answers; it told us we were in trouble but it never really defined the trouble or what its origins were; at its best its prescriptions were vague and elusive (obviously there was an allergy to concreteness); at its worst they were nonexistent.

From the reaction the report engendered you would predict that it would be followed by some kind of action. If the nation was at risk, should not steps be taken to minimize the risk? For all practical purposes nothing happened; the risk has increased, not decreased. President Reagan was no activist; he had not appointed a commission whose members' credentials indicated that they had firsthand knowledge of classrooms, schools, school systems, preparatory programs, and the recent history of educational reform. The president did not pose concrete questions that any thoughtful person might ask about a major and intractable social-institutional problem. Yes, I am saying that President Reagan was not thoughtful, a characterization already foreshadowed by what he said about education in the 1980 presidential campaign—that is, that eliminating the Department of Education would go a long way toward improving the quality of education. That made as much sense as President Carter's assertion that by creating a department to oversee education he was taking a necessary and bold step on the road to educational reform.

Obviously, I do not believe that commissioned reports by presidents and others in high office can be counted on to be productive. But there are enough instances to justify saying that when such political leaders ask concrete questions that require concrete answers, when asking reflects a sincere curiosity as well as a willingness to inform the public, when the seriousness of the problem is recognized despite the political uncertainties a report may create—when luck is on our side and there is a coincidence of these factors, we stand a chance of unimprisoning ourselves from mindless practice and those silent axioms we so take for granted that we can never examine them. But no president has seen fit to ask the likes of Darling-Hammond to do what she and her colleagues have done so well in regard to one aspect of educational reform that, if left undiscussed and unchanged, will defeat any effort at meaningful reform.

In the game of blame assignment for our educational ills only one stakeholder has been spared: the president. Is that not strange? After all, if concern for our schools is no longer a transient affair, is it not because our presidents and others in high office have told us we should be concerned, even though many people did not need to be told to be concerned? And, in addition, to those who reached adulthood in the post–World War II era, has it not been obvious that no president can claim that anything he has said and done was a difference that made a difference? I know it sounds harsh, but I feel justified in saying that the day is past when the failure of a president's policies—inaction and tepid actions are policies—should not be called just that: a failure cloaked in empty rhetoric about what we owe children and our societal traditions. At the same time it is obvious that the president does not know the difference between an assumption and a fact. What presidents have had to say about education exposes the cavernous depths of their ignorance. Their ignorance is so inexcusably vast as to guarantee that the more they seek to change things the more things will remain the same.

I postponed writing this book because I felt that what I had to say required that I go over ground covered in my books of recent years. The prospect of doing that was too daunting. What helped change my mind was the realization that nobody with whom I talked regarded schools generally with anything like approval. Also, in recent years I have asked people whom I meet the following question: If you were starting from scratch, would you come up with the kind of system we now have? Nobody answered in the affirmative. What came to mystify me was that nobody blamed political leaders (even in small measure) for the inadequacies of our schools and for failure of the expenditure of billions upon billions of dollars to have a desirable effect. Was it that people thought the substantive problems were so arcane and complex that we should not expect, say, a president to comprehend them sufficiently to be able to say or do anything appropriate, informative, provocative? Finally I realized that whenever a president said something about education, the need for sleep would overtake me. I expected absolutely nothing from presidents, although in regard to other major social problems I and others expect, at the least, evidence that a president was engaged in learning something. A president who does not learn or lead should not be exempt from criticism, however caustic. In regard to educational reform our recent presidents have neither learned nor led. Posterity will not treat them kindly.

After this book was completed and in production, there appeared in all the mass media the results of the Third International Mathematics and Science Study, involving large samples of fourth and eighth graders in a variety of countries. Two findings were emphasized:

- American fourth-grade students outperformed all but Korean and Japanese students in science. The Korean average was 597, the Japanese average 574, and the American 565. The average for all countries was 524.
- American fourth-grade students were outperformed by seven countries in math. Singapore scored best with 625. The overall average was 529; the United States average was 565.

From the president on down the political hierarchy, these results were greeted with enthusiastic gratification. President Clinton said, "The report proves that we don't have to settle for second-class expectations or second-class goals." Secretary Riley said, "Our elementary schools are getting better at teaching the basics."

What about eighth graders? As the *New York Times* (June 11, 1997) described it, there was "a mysterious sag in [American] students' relative skills by eighth grade." President Clinton noted that the American students did not sustain their early success, which, he said, means "we are doing a very good job in the early grades but we have got a lot more work to do in the later ones."

Is it being overly critical to say that the president should have known, or should have been told by his educational advisers, that waxing enthusiastic about one test given at one point in time may be somewhat premature, that there have been previous instances where early gains (or what appeared to be gains) did not hold up over time—as in the case of Head Start, where early findings became less and less robust. (Ed Zigler, one of Head Start's founders, was more than bothered by political leaders who did not want to listen to his advice about caution.) And as I emphasize in this book and previous ones, is it not noteworthy that as students go from elementary to middle to high school their level of boredom and disinterest increases? Is that unrelated to the sag in eighth-grade results?

Is it also hypercritical to expect that political leaders should have learned the difference between a longitudinal study, where you follow the same students over time, as in the case of many Head Start studies, and a cross-sectional study, where at each point of testing the students are different? Yes, I expect that a political leader who is seriously interested in improving schools will have made it his or her business to learn, among other things, that conclusions drawn from longitudinal studies have a practical importance, both for policy and practice, that cross-sectional studies do not have. Many political leaders grasp this point in relation to understanding health-medical problems; they have strongly supported such longitudinal studies as the Framingham health project, which has paid handsome dividends. No, I do not expect political leaders to become scholars or experts on education. But if those leaders unanimously agree that improving the quality of our schools is crucial, a must, a number one national priority, they should feel obligated to learn more than they do. As I indicate in this book, the last serious education president this country has had was Thomas Jefferson, and I devote many pages to the personal attention he gave to education. He did not limit himself to focusing on what others said or did or did not do. On his own, he thought, probed, and acted. In the post–World War II era, when education steadily became a source of national concern, no president or other political leader in high office has even remotely shown such interest in and knowledge of education.

The response to the recent International Mathematics and Science Study is but one example of what I critique in this book. I can assure the reader that I know that the arena of education is a very complex one, to indulge understatement. But as I said earlier, I find it strange that in the fruitless game of blame assignment, the roles and obligations of political leaders have hardly been examined. In fact, some leaders have made blame assignment fashionable, a point I discuss in the pages of this book. No one in or out of the educational community has willed the present situation. There are no villains. But we have yet to take seriously the possibility that our educational system is one incapable of reforming itself, a system whose undergirding axioms, organizational style, and practices are self-defeating of its purposes. That possibility is, as I will discuss later, implied (it is never explicit) in the call for charter schools by presidents and governors. But those and other political leaders stop short of recognizing that in calling for charter schools they are suggesting that the present system is unrescuable—that school change cannot take place within the system, only outside it. But, as I will relate, the outcome of the charter school movement is very iffy, and we will never know why some charter schools achieve some of their goals and others (a majority) do not.

I did not write this book to blame political leaders but rather because they are part of the educational system—a very crucial part—and, therefore, have to be held accountable in the same way and for the same reasons they hold school personnel accountable—that is, what they do or do not do should be scrutinized and judged. We expect presidents and others to learn, to want to learn about issues for which they propose action. In regard to educational reform they have learned little, if anything. They are grossly ahistorical; their conception of the learning process is one of "shape up or ship out"; and their sense and knowledge of the culture of classrooms, schools, and school systems virtually nonexistent. That sounds harsh, I know, but I ask the reader to reserve judgment until after the book has been read.

Before concluding this preface, I wish to devote a few words to Albert Shanker, who died on February 22, 1997. Nothing I say in Chapters Five and Six should obscure the fact that he played a major, positive role in changing the power relations among teachers, administrators, and policymakers. Most people do not know or do not remember that teachers used to be regarded as servants. Indeed, they were treated as I have said too many students feel teachers treat them. Shanker's militant, charismatic leadership—first in the New York local and then as national president—changed all that. But he did more than fight for higher salaries (which had been absurdly low) and better working conditions. Up until the past several years he used his office and *New York Times* column to identify and illuminate crucial professional-conceptual issues, and I came to respect him highly. No one more than he in the educational community in the post–World War II era developed and sustained the attention of a national audience. We met several times, each time for several hours. Not only was he amazingly bright and knowledgeable—as intellectually quick as they come—but he truly understood education as a system. He knew far more about how the system works than was reflected in his speeches and writings. I am sure that when his biography is written—and it should be written—the dimensions of his contributions will be apparent. I always felt—and still feel—uncomfortable disagreeing with him, but I was always aware that he could take care of himself in any argument. He was formidable. He was also a nice guy.

Finally, I am indebted to the Bellagio Study and Conference Center of the Rockefeller Foundation for a month's stay in February 1997, during which time this book was finished. The unrivaled beauty of the center on Italy's Lake Como is initially an obstacle even to getting started on your work, but well-deserved feelings of guilt soon obtrude and dominate, and for several hours each day you willingly submit to the tyranny of such feelings so that you can truly enjoy for a few hours the loveliest scenes and vistas you have ever seen. As always, I express my deepest gratitude and enduring affection for Lisa Pagliaro, who makes sense of my handwriting. Why learn to use a word processor if it means that I will not have contact with the likes of Lisa?

Stratford, Connecticut   SEYMOUR B. SARASON
December 1997

The Author

Seymour B. Sarason is professor of psychology emeritus in the Department of Psychology and at the Institute for Social and Policy Studies at Yale University. He founded, in 1962, and directed, until 1970, the Yale Psycho-Educational Clinic, one of the first research and training sites in community psychology. He received his Ph.D. (1942) from Clark University and holds honorary doctorates from Syracuse University, Queens College, Rhode Island College, and Lewis and Clark College. He has received an award for distinguished contributions to the public interest and several awards from the divisions of clinical and community psychology of the American Psychological Association, as well as two awards from the American Association on Mental Deficiency.

Sarason is the author of numerous books and articles. His more recent books include *The Making of an American Psychologist: An Autobiography* (1980); *The Predictable Failure of Educational Reform: Can We Change Course Before It's Too Late?* (1990); *The Challenge of Art to Psychology* (1990); *You Are Thinking of Teaching? Opportunities, Problems, Realities* (1993); *The Case for Change: Rethinking the Preparation of Educators* (1993); *Letters to a Serious Education President* (1993); *Psychoanalysis, General Custer, and the Verdicts of History and Other Essays on Psychology in the Social Scene* (1994); *Parental Involvement and the Political Principle: Why the Existing Governance Structure of Schools Should Be Abolished* (1995); and *Barometers of Change: Individual, Educational, and Social Transformation* (1996).

Political Leadership and Educational Failure

Chapter One

| Presidential Leadership

If tomorrow we were told that a cure for the most frequent type of cancer had been found, there would be no doubt that means for providing the cure to afflicted individuals would shortly follow. And that would also be the case if a cure for AIDS was found. When a vaccine to prevent polio was validated, the question was how fast the vaccine could be administered to at-risk populations; institutional and financial considerations were no barrier. No one needed to be convinced that the elimination of polio would be a dream come true. No one more than President Franklin Roosevelt ensured that the citizenry would know what polio did to individuals and families. A polio victim himself, he started the March of Dimes Foundation to support research and modes of treatment. If he used himself, his office, and the foundation for these purposes (including public education), it was because of personal experience. He did not learn about polio from his advisers; he had experienced the scourge of polio. Contrast that to what he advocated for the economy during the presidential campaign in 1931 and what he advocated to address the Great Depression after he was inaugurated in 1932. During the campaign he ran on a platform that was not dramatically less conservative than that of his opponent, President Hoover. Roosevelt came from a patrician family—he never experienced financial insecurity, he had never been jobless, let alone without food. He had no basis for comprehending the significance of the 1929 stock market crash and the economic depression, which was to be labeled the Great Depression. By the time he took office he realized how wrong he had been about both the causes and implications of the catastrophe. He and his advisers (called the "Brain Trust") devised a variety of programs to stem the tide, which with a few exceptions (supervision of financial markets, social security, conservation) were ineffective. In fact, during his first two terms the depression deepened; what he thought to be temporary measures, forms of Band-Aids, could no longer be so regarded. What brought the Great Depression to an end were the clouds of war in Europe, our beginning to rearm, the outbreak of war in Europe, and then our entry into war on December 7, 1941.

If Roosevelt and his advisers had misdiagnosed the whys of the Great Depression, and if their programs were ineffective, his critics had nothing to offer except to insist that Roosevelt was trampling on the traditions that had made the country great. They saw Roosevelt as intent on scuttling the capitalist system and its ethos of rugged individualism. They fought him tooth and nail. (The Social Security Act passed by one vote.) Whatever they were in their private lives, they were amazingly uncaring and uncompassionate to the plight of twenty million citizens who were jobless, despairing, and facing a bleak future. At least Roosevelt radiated compassion and hope and a willingness to experiment in order to come up with more effective reforms. Marie Antoinette said of the hungry, rebellious people of Paris that if they did not have bread, "let them eat cake." Roosevelt's critics did not go that far, although the millions of unemployed saw the critics as advocating just that.

What enabled Roosevelt to convince the nation that he knew what they were experiencing, even if he could not explain why the catastrophe occurred and why it was not as short-lived as he had said and hoped? Certainly among the complex of factors in any answer to that question is his wife, Eleanor, one of the most remarkable women in American history. Not only did she travel around the country observing, listening, talking, but she communicated her experiences forthrightly and persistently to her husband. The line between persistence and needling was a fine one. If his background provided no personal basis for comprehending what suffering millions were thinking and feeling, Eleanor provided one such basis.[1]

If the New Deal programs were far from effective in terminating the depression, they were very effective in a psychological-

---

1.   Her role as the president's eyes and ears among the people is very well described in Goodwin (1994).

humanitarian sense in that they prevented mass hunger, provided work opportunities for jobless young and older people (including artists of all kinds), and prevented that level of hopelessness that could lead to civil unrest or rebellion. Those achievements would not have been possible without the leadership of a man and his wife who knew what millions of people were thinking and feeling. If Hoover had been reelected, the subsequent history of this country would have been quite different, and it is not unwarranted to speculate that that history would have been to no one's liking.

Roosevelt considered legislation that would be a form of universal health insurance. Because of the strength of the opposition to the Social Security Act, he decided that to propose health insurance would endanger passage of the Social Security Act, and it went on a back burner that never got lit. I have no evidence that his interest in health insurance in part derived from personal experience with the financial and psychological consequences of chronic, handicapping illness. Nonetheless, however financially secure he was, he must have known that the costs of his illness were fantastically beyond the means of all but an insignificant number of people.

These introductory remarks have several implications. First, unlike cures for serious and widespread illness and disease, efforts to repair or prevent societally destabilizing problems encounter formidable institutional and psychological opposition. Longstanding attitudes, traditions, and institutional inertia guarantee opposition. To expect otherwise is to believe in secular miracles or to be wedded to a psychology that has not a shred of confirming evidence in human history. Second, the leadership of a social change effort, if it is to be even partially effective, must at the very least possess and convey understanding of how those who are the objects of change think and feel. That depth of understanding may derive from personal experience or from relationships that compensate for lack of personal experience. Either way, the leadership has to convey empathy and concrete understanding—not abstractions, euphemisms, generalities, or any other form empty rhetoric may take. Third, even where criteria for the first two points are met, it does not necessarily follow that the chosen course of action will have its intended outcomes. To understand how people think and feel is a form of identification—that is, it is a use of personal experience to discern commonalities. But the recognition of those commonalities may tell one little or nothing about how to change contexts so that people will henceforth think and feel in more productive and satisfying ways. Beyond commonalities is the question of etiology: What are the features of the social context that cause people to be unhappy, ineffective, and derogated, and to feel victimized? Put in another way: There is a difference between a reform effort that is a form of palliative and a reform effort that is powered by a conception of why and how the undesirable state of affairs comes about. That conception, I hasten to add, may or may not be justified by available evidence; indeed, in the realm of social affairs subsequent experience very frequently proves such conceptions to be unjustified. Opposition to an effort at social change arises from widely (and sometimes wildly) differing conceptions of etiology (welfare reform is a clear instance).

The overarching thrust of what I have said is quite obvious. In regard to the most pressing social problems it is a difference that makes a difference who is in the role of president, or governor, or in some other clearly powerful political role. That is a glimpse of the obvious. What is not obvious is that the verdicts of history are uncomfortably and frequently damning of eras in which leaders and most of the people either ignored, misunderstood, or mishandled social problems that over time had untoward consequences. We like to believe that in the present era we have identified the most important problems, and we can point to polls that tell us how people rank the seriousness of these problems, rankings influenced by what political leaders say. But identification of a problem and its ranking do not mean we understand it in any etiological sense. Indeed, if we know anything, it is that for any of these major problems different individuals and groups have very differing understandings that lead to very different courses of action. And we know one other thing: for most if not all of these problems (for example, drugs, welfare dependency, crime, violence, teenage pregnancy), none of the different courses of action has been more than minimally effective, if at all effective. If these problems deserve any label, it is *intractable*. Intractability is a sure sign that our understanding of a problem is grievously in error in some important respect. Political leaders cannot say that a problem is intractable or that their understanding is incomplete or fuzzy. They must appear to understand and to know what to do. Posterity is the cruelest of critics—future generations will give short shrift to past leaders and peoples who did not know they did not know but could have known what needed to be done in regard to major problems. And that is the point: future historians will very likely be able to point to individuals in our era whose understanding correctly predicted what, so to speak, would be coming down the road and why. It will not be a case of twenty-twenty hindsight. In our national history slavery is the clearest example.

In a book of essays titled *Jefferson, Nationalism and the Enlightenment*, Commager (1975) discusses the basis of Jefferson's explicit opposition to slavery. Here are some of Jefferson's words:

> There must doubtless be an unhappy influence on the manners of our people produced by the existence of slavery among us. The whole commerce between master and slave is a perpetual exercise of the most boisterous passions, the most unremitting despotism on the one part, and degrading submissions on the other. Our children see this and learn to imitate it. . . . The parent storms, the child looks on, catches the lineaments of wrath, puts on the same airs in the circle of smaller slaves, gives a loose to the worst of passions, and thus nursed, educated, and daily exercised in tyranny, cannot but be stamped by it with odious peculiarities. The man must be a prodigy who can retain his manners and morals undepraved by such circumstances. And with what execration should the statesman be loaded who, permitting one half the citizens to trample on the rights of the other, transforms those into despots, and these into enemies, destroys the morals of the one part and the *amor patriae* of the other. . . . With the morals of the people, their industry is also destroyed. For in a warm climate no man will labor for himself who can make another labor for him. . . . And can the liberties of a nation be thought secure when we have removed their only firm basis, a conviction in the minds of the people that these liberties are of the gift of God? That they are not to be violated but with His wrath? Indeed I tremble for my country when I reflect that God is just; that his justice cannot sleep forever; that considering numbers, nature and natural means only, a revolution of the wheel of fortune, an exchange of situation, is among possible events; that it may become probable by supernatural interference. The Almighty has no attribute which can take side with us in such a contest [p. 56].

Like others of his time Jefferson opposed slavery on both moral and religious grounds, but his opposition was much more nuanced than that, and much more prophetic and powerful. His psychological understanding of the master-slave relationship, be it among children or adults, pierces the overt veneer of that relationship and exposes the volcanic passions inevitably elicited both in master and slave, passions that ensure that if and when the unpredictable "wheel of fortune" alters circumstances those passions will erupt with destructive force. That kind of understanding is not attainable unless to some degree an individual (like Jefferson) has himself experienced those passions, and has the courage to admit it *and* to draw the appropriate conclusions. Jefferson was not alone in asserting that all humans had identical capacities to experience love, joy, hate, shame, guilt, and so forth, but he went beyond that generalization to conclude that the master-slave relationship poisoned both parties and essentially was destroying and would consume them both. And that was true for adults and children, and in regard to the latter he describes the process in amazingly few words, just as Rodgers and Hammerstein did in the song in *South Pacific*: "You have to be taught to love and hate, you have to be taught before you are eight." The young black slave and young white master learned to hate long before they were eight.

I am no historian of slavery in colonial times but from what I have read it was Jefferson who had the most sophisticated understanding of why slavery had the potential of destroying the country.[2] The Civil War settled the legal issue but little else. It could be (and has been) argued that it is misleading and unfair to judge the distant past by today's values and knowledge. That it can be misleading and unfair I quite agree. But the point I am emphasizing is that Jefferson's insight has not been recognized or assimilated by many people today. There are whites who cannot comprehend why blacks continue to express or harbor feelings of anger and hatred toward—and mistrust of—them. There are blacks for whom it is axiomatic that whites—regardless of what they say or do—are

---

2.   I am aware that although Jefferson understood the poisonous consequences of slavery, he also held less commendable views characteristic of people in the South (O'Brien, 1996). Arkes (1997) casts Jefferson's less commendable views in a different light, as does Bowman (1997).

neither sincere nor to be trusted.[3] Jefferson would have understood both groups because he knew that attitudes and feelings honed over the centuries will take centuries to change, if then.

Political leaders, we are told, have the responsibility to proclaim a moral vision that inspires the citizenry with feelings of national purpose, cohesiveness, and transcendence. I quite agree. But in regard to some major problems, inspiring is not enough; inspiration will not suffice for a problem that has been intransigent to reform, or that will require unlearning old attitudes and acquiring new ones, or that will require a new effort the substance and justifications of which will have to be described concretely. Putting it that way implies that the leader has come to an understanding not possessed by people generally, in which case he or she faces two related questions: "Do I truly lead, knowing ahead of time that what I will be saying and advocating will not be met with approval, let alone enthusiasm, in some quarters?" "Instead of leading do I follow; do I recommend a course of action consistent with the way most people view the problem, even though I have reason to believe that course of action will not be effective?" The first question raises the communication problem: the leader must describe the changed view of the problem so that the explanation has meaning in people's experience—they will take action only if they hear something to which they can relate personally. The second question raises what I call the myth of uniqueness: the change in the leader's thinking is not one people in general will be able to understand; they will oppose it and the leader will be isolated, so it may seem better to play it safe and stay within the confines of what people now think and feel.

There are three preconditions that make a leader a leader. The first is that he or she concludes that the particular social problem is so serious as to endanger the social fabric, slowly perhaps, but with a predictably increasing pace. The second is that the leader assumes that describing and communicating the process by which

---

3.   The racial issue is more complicated than I can indicate here. The point I am emphasizing is that each era has blind spots that, except for a few individuals, prevent understanding why certain major social problems appear to be intractable. This point, I hope, will become clearer when we discuss the failures of educational reform.

his or her thinking changed will strike responsive chords in many people. The third is that the leader knows there will be opposition, very strong opposition, but sees that as no reason for not giving currency to his or her beliefs, fears, and initial proposals for action.

What is the relevance of what I have said to the goal of improving our educational system? I have written about our schools in earlier publications (Sarason, 1982, 1983, 1990, 1992, 1993b, 1995b, 1996b, 1997), and I cannot present my point of view here in detail. Besides, as I hope to make clear in subsequent chapters, this book rests on the belief that unless and until those who occupy the highest elected public offices change their accustomed way of defining the problem of school change, the level and quality of educational outcomes will continue their downward course with disruptive consequences signifying that the American promise has become at best empty rhetoric and at worst a societal nightmare. Ironically, the redefinition that is necessary does not require arcane knowledge, which is not to suggest that the application of that knowledge is a simple affair.

We have in our lives experienced the differences between contexts of productive and unproductive learning. We know when we have been turned on or off. We know when ideas and concepts have taken on meaning for and application to personal experiences. We know when what we have been asked or required to learn compels us to substitute memorization for understanding, when questions about "why to learn" are answered in terms of a distant future we can neither comprehend nor envision, when our concrete questions and puzzlements remain private for fear of exposing ignorance followed by derogation. Likewise, we know when we come alive because our individuality is recognized and supported—that is, when we are not perceived in terms of categories in which our individuality does not exist and the characteristics of which allow others to see us as a part of a collection of people to whom a homogeneity is attributed that is unjustified, invalid, and makes a mockery of the concept of individuality.

Because I cannot go over ground covered in detail in other publications, I shall now in a series of bare-bones statements give the basis for why in this book I shall argue that efforts to improve our schools will go nowhere unless and until political leadership redefines the problem in terms of the differences between contexts of productive and unproductive learning. Many readers will be puzzled about why I place such a responsibility on political leaders who, they will contend, are unsophisticated (to say the least) about the whys and wherefores of the educational process and context. That contention assumes that the educational community should have the major responsibility for the redefinition process. The brute fact is that far from assuming that responsibility the educational community has bulwarked the status quo, obscuring the necessity for the redefinition process. But what I must emphasize at this point is that the substance and justification of the redefinition process is knowable both to the educational community and to the political leadership in that they already know from personal experience the difference between contexts of productive and unproductive learning. What both have been unable to do is to apply that personally derived knowledge to the stultifying realities of classrooms and schools and drawing the appropriate conclusions.

Anything important I have ever said or written has been said by others today and in the near and distant past. I claim no originality whatsoever. Ironically, whenever I have presented my analysis of why the reform movement has failed and will continue to fail—in scores of presentations to groups of educators and so-called lay people—no one, but no one, has ever voiced disagreement. At best, I am told I am a visionary; at worst, I am labeled a utopian living in a world of my own—that is, impractical. When I respond by saying that in the post–World War II era nothing has been more pragmatically impractical than the reform movement, nobody disagrees and nobody offers an alternative that is essentially other than a retread of what has failed in the past. Today we hear a good deal about vouchers, charter schools, privatization, and the potentials of modern technology. Since it is hard to be completely wrong, I have to say that for each of these there is (or may be) a kernel of truth. For reasons contained in what follows, however, the kernels of truth they may contain will have no general, practical consequences.

• To claim that in the post–World War II era there have not been scores upon scores of well-intentioned, well-funded reform efforts is inexcusably and irresponsibly ahistorical. Similarly, to assert that these efforts have had their intended generalized effects is to confuse reality with wish fulfillment, or worse.

- Up until a decade or so ago, many educators, political leaders, and members of the general public believed that increasing funding for schools would raise the level and quality of educational outcomes. Few believe that any longer. For example, the city of Hartford, in an act of desperation, gave over (for a time) its educational system to a private company. That system was, is, and will continue to be an educational disaster even despite the fact that per-pupil expenditure is second in Connecticut only to a Fairfield County community populated by Wall Street executives and their peers. In this respect, Hartford is not an atypical American city.

- Not long after the end of World War II, the federal government dramatically departed from a tradition almost totally limiting any role in education for that government. The reason for that departure was the recognition of the inability of cities to cope with the needs and deficits of their school systems (see Sarason, 1996a, pp. 91–92). With each passing year the gulf between cities and suburbs in regard to any criterion of educational quality and outcome has widened. Educators know that—and so do many political leaders, some of whom have explicitly said that cities are social time bombs whose potential for societal destabilization is vastly underestimated.

- If there is anything that an extraterrestrial humanoid would conclude from observing American society in regard to schools, it is that the sole criterion for judging schools is whether test scores go up or down or remain the same. Whether the test scores have any relationship to productive learning, or whether they reflect drill and memorization, is ignored. Test scores are thermometers of educational health or illness. It is like saying that the size and changes in the measures of Gross National Product are unambiguous in regard to economic health even though those measures include the activities of companies dealing directly or indirectly with research and treatment of cancer, AIDS, alcoholism, smoking, illicit drugs, and scores of other conditions.

- The reform movement has been near exclusively a repair effort. Prevention is hardly in the picture, the conventional rhetoric notwithstanding. Initially, Head Start was a preventive effort: the inoculation of at-risk preschoolers against the viruses of poor school performance and reduced motivation. Although Head Start has had some positive effects, no one claims that the effects are robust enough to counter what these children experience in the modal classroom.

• As children go from the elementary to the middle to the high school (those who get that far), the level of motivation and interest in school learning decreases, a fact well known to middle and high school teachers, many of whom over time experience burnout or begin to look forward to retirement, or both.

• For all practical purposes the reform movement has been preoccupied with the elementary school. Middle and high schools are perceived (as they should be) as being too large, too complicated, too inflexible to be amenable to other than cosmetic changes. What few efforts have been mounted to change these schools are not inspiring, although they have had the important virtue of illuminating what should be done.

• It is not surprising that some reformers look upon the use of modern technology as a kind of universal solvent for the fecklessness of schools, just as there were people (not including Edward Zigler, one of the founders of Head Start) who saw or hoped that Head Start would be a major breakthrough. The most recent example is the "Summit Conference" convened with much fanfare by Louis Gerstner, CEO of IBM. The report emanating from that conference—as I have analyzed and discussed elsewhere (Sarason, 1997)—is inexcusably ahistorical, acultural, and (to be charitable) superficial.

• Anxiety about our schools is reflected in two questions: How did the problem come to be as serious as it is? Who is responsible—that is, who should be held accountable? For most people the second question contains the answer to the first. (It does not, but that is another story I cannot go over again here.) The fact is that the governance system of education makes assignment of accountability virtually impossible. The governance system is no simple affair. It consists of teachers, educational administrators, boards of education, the state departments of education, the legislative and executive branches of state and federal government, parents, and colleges and universities. It is an uncoordinated system the parts of which are not and cannot be in agreement about any one overarching purpose of education. Informally, it is an adversarial system

(Sarason, 1996a). It is not a system that has ever faced and reached agreement about the nature of and differences between contexts of productive and unproductive learning.

• You can find a classroom here and a classroom there, a school here and a school there (almost always an elementary school) where the differences between productive and unproductive learning are taken seriously. You cannot find a school district about which that can be said. The exceptions exist despite rather than because of the system. These exceptions do not spread beyond their narrow confines. The existing system of governance does not learn from exceptions; it does not seek or does not know how to capitalize on them. It is not a self-correcting, self-improving system.

Satire captures some aspects of some of these points, which is why I give (again) the "Horse Story," written by an unknown author and left in the mailbox of Professor Emory Cowen of the University of Rochester.

Horse Story

Common advice from knowledgeable horse trainers includes the adage, *"If the horse you're riding dies, get off."* Seems simple enough, yet in the education business we don't always follow that advice. Instead, we often choose from an array of alternatives that includes:

1. Buying a stronger whip.
2. Trying a new bit or bridle.
3. Switching riders.
4. Moving the horse to a new location.
5. Riding the horse for longer periods of time.
6. Saying things like, "This is the way we've always ridden this horse."
7. Appointing a committee to study the horse.
8. Arranging to visit other sites where they ride dead horses efficiently.
9. Increasing the standards for riding dead horses.
10. Creating a test for measuring our riding ability.
11. Comparing how we're riding now with how we did ten or twenty years ago.
12. Complaining about the state of horses these days.

13. Coming up with new styles of riding.
14. Blaming the horse's parents. The problem is often in the breeding.
15. Tightening the cinch.

I have one quarrel with the "Horse Story": it places blame on educators. From my perspective, educators are only one part, albeit a very important part, of the overall system—they are far from the only ones who have been unable to take seriously what they know from personal and professional experience. Schools are to their inhabitants uninteresting, unstimulating, impersonal places where respect for individuality is rarely found—or even possible. Contexts for productive learning do not exist for teachers. *When those contexts do not exist for teachers, teachers cannot create and sustain those contexts for students.* I regard that as a glimpse of the obvious, and in an inchoate way teachers know that. And, in my experience, that is also known to political leaders, again in an inchoate way.

Some readers will find themselves continuing to ask why I am giving a key role to leaders at the highest level of elected political office. I shall endeavor to answer that question in detail in the next chapter. Let me here emphasize that these leaders are quite capable of comprehending the differences between contexts of productive and unproductive learning in terms of their own experiences in school and elsewhere. Few people have disputed my assertion that their school experience contained few occasions that stimulated them, energized them, made them desirous to learn more, in small or large ways changed them, and were associated with a sense of personal and intellectual growth; such instances were indeed the polar opposite of the great bulk of their school experience. There is, however, another reason for my emphasis: the substance and dimensions of the problem are such that only the president and a few others can begin the process whereby the problem and its implications for action can be brought to national attention. The problem is not a local one. The problem can be put this way: How can we take seriously what we know, what in fact has been demonstrated here and there but has not spread elsewhere, so that our purposes will have a more general acceptance and appropriate implementation? And let us not forget that some (not a few) of those "here and there" demonstrations have had a short life precisely because of institutional traditions and barriers. Why do bad things happen to good people? The system of governance and the culture of the school provide the answers (Sarason, 1996a, 1997).

An Addendum: In the 1960s, many cities adopted Project Concern, a program in which inner-city youngsters were bussed to suburban schools. It was a program that encountered silent and vocal opposition. In many cases the program was adopted reluctantly and because of social unrest in cities that the suburbs could not ignore—that is, there were more than a few suburban residents who felt a moral obligation to do *something*. From whatever I learned in those years there was no evidence that Project Concern would achieve its goals; a conclusion that subsequent years confirmed. I was then director of the Yale Psycho-Educational Clinic. I was told that Project Concern in Hartford was going well and, indeed, that a formal evaluation had been done by Dr. Thomas Mahan of the University of Hartford, whom I then knew slightly. I invited him to make a presentation, which he based on data subsequently published. It was a heartening discussion because Dr. Mahan described in detail how he had directed and evaluated Project Concern. It was quite a story, told by someone who knew schools and communities.

While working on this chapter I wrote a personal note to Dr. Mahan, who had taken a position at The Citadel in Charleston, South Carolina, after he left Hartford. In the course of the letter I asked him if his evaluation had been published and what had happened thereafter. Here is the relevant paragraph from his reply:

> Your note referred to the *real* data which we published on Project Concern in 1966–68. We did indeed have such real data and the Rand Corporation (Dr. Robert Crain) did a 15 year later follow-up study which demonstrated in almost all spheres the benefit of the experience for these Hartford kids. Alas, by then the powers-that-be had first emasculated and then closed the project! That seems to be a recurring theme in my career—the program in Charleston which I shared with you (Project Challenge) withered and died after I retired. Your message on person-dependent interventions is a painful one.

Dr. Mahan's experience is one of those "here and there" educational accomplishments that the governance of our educational system is unable to learn from and to exploit. Faced with such an instance, people in the system invariably make decisions unwittingly calculated to confirm the maxim that no good deed goes unpunished.

Chapter Two

What Politicians Know but Cannot Apply

Not long after World War II began, a refugee physicist, Leo Szilard, understood the military-political implications of recent experiments demonstrating that atoms had been split with a release of energy of potentially galactic proportions—that is, an atomic bomb could become a reality. The experiments were known throughout the international community of physicists, which meant that German physicists could provide Hitler, who already appeared unstoppable, with a weapon that would ensure him victory. Szilard agonized as to how to get this information to President Roosevelt so that he would approve the long and costly process enabling America to have the bomb before the Germans. It was Szilard who prevailed on Albert Einstein to write a letter to the president stating why the country should move to capitalize on this new knowledge. The president acted. He was not a physicist; he was incompetent to judge whether the experiments were well designed and their conclusions and implications justified. But he knew two things. He knew his country was in mortal danger, and he knew that if the preeminent physicist in the world testified to the validity and implications of these scientific demonstrations, he had to take it most seriously. Einstein was not telling him what *might* happen *if* the atom *could* be split but that the atom had been split—that is, what had been a theoretical possibility was now a practical reality.

The point of this anecdote is that only the president could have taken the appropriate action. It does not follow, of course, that any person in the Oval Office would have had the wisdom and courage to make that decision. Long before most people, including political leaders, Roosevelt clearly understood the threat of German Nazism. Indeed, he was accused of wanting to get his country to take sides even before the war formally erupted in 1939. What was indubitably true was that Roosevelt assumed the moral and educational responsibility to get the people to begin to confront the consequences of a German victory. He knew there would be a day of reckoning and if we put our heads in the sand, we might end up with no heads at all.

We do not expect presidents to comprehend the substantive ins and outs of all major problems with which they must deal, any more than Roosevelt had to understand how to split the atom. But we do (or should) expect two things. First, the president should have made the most serious effort to weigh and judge the societal consequences of not dealing forthrightly with a problem—that is, not all problems are equally serious in their societal consequences. Second, in regard to the most serious problems we expect the president to tell us if implemented solutions have not been effective, are not effective, and will continue to be ineffective—and why. We expect the president to answer the why question in these instances so that people have a basis of judging whether any new initiative holds out a promise of making an intractable problem tractable. Presidents (especially) are both followers and leaders. They must have a sense of what people think and feel at the same time they seek to stimulate them in ways that enlarge their knowledge and understanding. Presidents who are primarily followers tend to end up as footnotes in history books. Presidents who are leaders have a more difficult time in office, because although they may be sensitive to and respectful of what people think and feel, they seek bridges between where people are and where the leader believes they ought to be heading. Such leaders are in principle and practice in the same position as the classroom teacher who understands that a context of productive learning is one in which the teacher-leader truly understands what learners know, think, feel—their attitudes, experiences, expectations, social-familial-neighborhood surround—and seeks ways to enlarge their understanding of themselves, their world, and diverse others.

It may seem outlandishly inappropriate to compare presidents and classroom teachers, but only if you see people in terms of labels and categories and not their daily practical means and ends.

The teacher is or should be both follower and leader. The teacher, like the president, assumes the obligation of following and that means being sensitive to and knowledgeable about where learners are. It does not mean seeing them as empty vessels or unformed organisms devoid of previous experience relevant to the substance and process of learning. It does not mean requiring them from day one to conform to and absorb a predetermined, calendar-driven body of knowledge and associated cognitive skills, as if no bridges exist or need to be constructed between the prescribed knowledge and skills on one hand, and the learner's experience, expectations, curiosities, questions, attitudes, and motivations on the other hand. To construct such a bridge is what the British teacher in *The King and I* meant when she told her Siamese students that her task was "getting to know you, getting to know all about you." She was not saying that from the stance of a social worker intent on getting a comprehensive life history but rather as a teacher who knew that before she began "to fill them up," educationally speaking, she had to know a good deal about them. She was, so to speak, following in order to discharge her obligation to lead. The construction of a bridge is not for the purpose of one-way travel but for willing, personally meaningful two-way travel. Constructing a bridge in the classroom is not the same as firing well-intentioned bullets of information from one point (the teacher) to another (the learner) on the invalid assumption that the information will or can be productively assimilated and a source of motivation to learn more.

In principle (that is, in the abstract), what I have just said is old hat to a president or others in very high elected office. It is second nature to them to seek ways of determining what their constituents are thinking, feeling, and expecting. Some of these officials, perhaps most of them, seek that information in order to avoid appearing at odds with their constituents even when the constituents do not seem to be seeing the issues in their complexity. Such officials follow their constituents; they do not seek to lead them, to begin the difficult (and dangerous) task of building a bridge with their constituents—that is, to seek to enlarge or change their outlook in some way. A far smaller number of officials have the courage to want to try to lead, not to be passive or mindless followers.

In the presidential election of 1948, every poll and so-called knowledgeable insider predicted that Thomas Dewey would handily defeat Harry Truman, who was running on a platform in the Franklin Roosevelt tradition, a platform considered radical in terms of economics and civil rights. Indeed, in the early edition of the *Chicago Tribune* on election night, even before all polling places had closed, the banner headline proclaimed Dewey's victory. What the experts were insensitive to was that the millions who came to vote were largely those with vivid memories of the Great Depression, of a business and manufacturing community for whom unions were anathema, of racial strife and riots, and more. Truman assumed he knew where the people were and to where they wanted to be led. It was the same Truman who performed one of the most courageous acts of this century even though he knew that, for a time at least, he would be tarred and feathered but in the long run would be praised, as he has been. I refer to his removal of General MacArthur, whose behavior challenged civilian control of the military.

The essential point is that politicians know that they have to begin with where their constituents are. They may be wrong both in the means they employ and the conclusions they draw—but they know where they have to begin. They know they cannot, must not, take those constituents for granted, especially if they have any ambition to be the type of leader who seeks to enlarge or change the perspective of the constituency in some way.

The most frequent and objective indices of the importance that officials give to probing what constituents think, feel, value, and expect are in the meteoric rise of polls and focus groups. The higher the stakes (and resources) the more frequently they are employed. There is a good news–bad news aspect to this development. The good news is that the politician believes, truly believes, that he or she must know what people are thinking, how they are reacting to messages that bombard them, and how they would or might react to an initiative the candidate considers important. It is good news because it illustrates and confirms an essential feature of a context of productive learning: before you lead (or teach), before you assume that your ends and means are those of others (students), before you assume that a bridge already exists between you and others, you *must* know where those others are coming from. The only thing you can take for granted is that if you ignore or short-circuit that feature, there very likely will be trouble ahead.

The bad news is that too often polls and focus groups are brief, impersonal one-time affairs involving no dialogue, no bridge building, no mutual learning. They are employed far more often than not for one purpose: to win, to be elected, to play it safe.

So what are the implications for the classroom teacher in an elementary school who is with the same group of children for most of the day and throughout the year? Are we justified to expect that the teacher has opportunity to know where the students are coming from? That the teacher wants to take advantage of that opportunity? The answer is yes and no. Let me elaborate by personal experience and a research study.

Decades ago, when I began to immerse myself in matters educational, I began to review my school years. There were two reasons stimulating that review. Sitting in and observing a wide variety of classrooms made it impossible to avoid the conclusion that classrooms were teacher centered, not student centered. Whatever went on was determined and directed and judged by the teacher. That, I should hasten to add, does not mean they were like army boot camps. Some were precisely that, but most were semi-relaxed, friendly places that nevertheless were indisputably teacher centered: the teacher was executive, legislature, and judiciary, and whatever discussion there was was initiated, directed, and controlled by the teacher. Teachers asked questions, students answered them. If the student was unable to answer or the answer was wrong, the teacher called on someone else. What I was seeing, in an attenuated form, was what John Dewey had described in 1899 in his presidential address to the American Psychological Association.

The second reason stimulating review of my school years was a traumatic event on the first day of a high school course in geometry, an event I have never forgotten and one that very much negatively influenced my attitude toward and competence in mathematics. At some point in that class the teacher went to the board, drew two connecting lines, and said, "That is an obtuse angle," and then went on to draw other types of angles. I panicked. What does obtuse mean? Where does such a word come from? What do you do with an obtuse angle? Why is this course called geometry? Was I the only one in the class who was in an anxious fog? No, I learned later, there were others in the same fog but *it could not occur to any of us to say out loud to the teacher what was in our heads*. We had to act as if we understood, we had to look interested, competent, "with it." We didn't want to appear dumb, no one of us wanted to be perceived as out in left field.

A group of colleagues and I did a study in which each of several assistants sat in a classroom for several of the beginning weeks of school.[1] Their task was to describe any instance relevant to the constitution of the classroom: the rules governing the behavior and obligations of everyone in that classroom—that is, how the rule was developed, who participated in the process, and the amount of time devoted to rule making. The long and short of it is that the observers had an easy time of it because there was no discussion of the whys and wherefores of rules. Either the constitution was presented by the teacher in ready-made form or the rules were stated by the teacher as instances relevant to them occurred. In no classroom did students participate in rule making or challenge a teacher-made rule. These observations are incomprehensible apart from any or all of the following assumptions:

- Students are indifferent to or uninterested in the rules by which they are governed or who makes the rules. (Most of the teachers were parents who knew better!)
- Students have no or little comprehension of the complexity of the relationship between rules and governance on one hand, and concepts of fairness and justice on the other hand. Therefore, to seek to involve them in some way in matters of governance is, to say the least, inadvisable and a waste of time.
- Students are in school to learn subject matter and associated skills. They may have questions and feelings about the whys and wherefores of learning subject matter but that is no warrant for taking valuable time to work through those questions and feelings. Some day in the future they will understand and judge favorably that teacher knew best.

---

1.   The study was reported in 1971 in the first edition of *The Culture of the School and the Problem of Change* (1982). In 1996 I was asked to revisit that book and add several chapters about if and how the classroom scene had changed. It has changed (here and there) but not much, and in regard to taking contexts of productive learning seriously, the change is minuscule in frequency.

- School is for intellectual-educational development, not personal development; you can foster the former without getting mired in the vagaries of the latter.
- Teachers have an overriding purpose. They are not psychologists, social workers, therapists, let alone the parents of their students. Of course students vary widely and wildly in regard to personal matters, but to surface and deal with those matters is not a teacher's obligation, besides which the teacher has no time to take individuality seriously.
- The attitudes elementary school children develop in regard to learning, subject matter, rules, teachers, and schools will positively influence their experience of middle and high school, even though those schools are larger than elementary schools and far more impersonal.

If presidents or any other elected public officials took what in principle would be an equivalent stance toward their constituents, they would not be in office very long. I write these words at the beginning of the presidential campaign of 1996. If there is anything the two candidates acknowledge and worry about, it is that people generally perceive Washington with distrust, cynicism, and anger. The use of the word *gridlock* has increased exponentially in frequency. It is far beyond my purposes to discuss or judge how the two candidates are responding but it is clearly relevant to my purposes simply to note the importance they give to seeking explanations of the whys and wherefores of what people are thinking and feeling. The candidates wish both to follow and to lead, especially when they hear the quip "Clinton does not deserve to be reelected and Dole does not deserve to win."

For two decades or so after World War II, the educational reform movement had a good deal of public support, monetarily and otherwise. It is a very different story today. It is not an exaggeration to say that many people have given up on the reform movement, and there are some who would not be unhappy to see the demise of public education as we have known it. They see the public school system as intractable and ineffective, and they see educators as self-serving and unimaginative. They are also puzzled about why so many students find school unchallenging, boring, uninteresting. Most people have no ready explanation—but when they hear the proposals of so-called experts, elected officials, and corporate types, they cannot generate hope or enthusiasm. Neither can I, if for only one reason: nobody talks about life in the modal classroom and whether those classrooms contain any of the features of the context of productive learning. They call for higher standards, greater expectations of students, more and better use of technology, and an end to promoting students who do not meet standards. In brief, there is nothing wrong with the system qua system that these alleged improvements will not remedy. However, unlike the earlier days after World War II, there are segments of the population, including some in the educational community, who have concluded that the present system is insensitive to or ignorant of what parents and students think, feel, need, and want. But even among those segments there is, for all practical purposes, no direct confrontation of the questions: What do we mean by a classroom context of productive learning? What has to begin to happen for such contexts to be approximated and to spread generally throughout our schools—not to be isolated "here and there" instances that may not (and usually do not) receive recognition and that may or may not survive? What is the starting point?

What I have been saying derives from my experience in elementary schools and a large observational and research literature that goes back a long way in time. I am saying nothing new. If I can claim any distinction it is that beginning in 1965, I predicted with 100 percent accuracy what would happen in our schools. That prediction was elaborated in my subsequent writings, which is why in 1990 I titled my book *The Predictable Failure of Educational Reform* and in 1993 I subtitled a book *Why the Existing Governance Structure of Schools Should Be Abolished.* If I were to go by the number and substance of letters I have received from teachers, parents, and an occasional principal, I would be justified in feeling encouraged. If I were to go by the impact of my writings on policymakers, I would be justified in feeling totally discouraged.

But I am not totally discouraged, for reasons I will give shortly. First let me make some brief comments about middle and high schools that someone said were major disaster areas. It is not happenstance that with very few exceptions reformers have steered clear of middle and high schools—there are diverse reasons, not the least of which are their size and bureaucratic features and departmental structure. Judged by criteria for contexts of productive learning these schools make elementary schools paragons of educational virtue. Although in terms of size and complexity middle and high schools are as nothing compared to the federal government, the reports from Vice President Gore's Reinventing Government initiative (1993a, 1993b) contain much relevant to those schools. I have discussed those reports elsewhere (Sarason and Lorentz, 1998), but it is useful to indicate several points here:

- Unlike every one of the scores of previous reports on improving government efficiency and service, the Gore reports are refreshingly candid, descriptively concrete, psychologically sophisticated and analytic, and diagnostically incisive and astute.
- The central question the reports ask is, What are the barriers to productive collaboration? Put in another way, why can't government agencies use their resources in ways that further their purposes to serve the public more sensitively, efficiently, and at less cost. Why is collaboration threatening and dangerous?
- Why do so many federal workers suffer from the "culture of futility"—that is, for them to engage in a change effort will confirm the adage that no good deed goes unpunished? It is somewhat amazing the degree to which the reports reflect a sensitivity to "where federal workers are" and why assigning blame to them is an egregious example of blaming the victim.
- What is required are new incentives that take into account what employees now think and feel, replacing the present formal and informal incentives that are antithetical to productive collaboration.
- To perceive federal employees as mindless drones unable to change or incompetent to participate in and contribute to collaborative decision making is to indulge and produce the worst features of the negative self-fulfilling prophecy.

All these points could be made and have been made in regard to middle and high schools. So, for example, many teachers feel that no one is truly interested in what they do, think, and would like to propose. They are quite aware of what the actuarial-educational data indicate: the more things change, the more they remain the same. Don't bang your head against a stone wall, act interested and engaged, take no chances because only your need for masochism will be gratified. By the time students get to high school they have been socialized to conform, keep quiet (most of the time), even though they will not get time off for good behavior. And how do many students feel when they finally graduate? They are *free*—and free means they stand a chance of feeling like and being treated like a person whose ideas, feelings, attitudes, hopes, and ambitions will not have to remain in an unwanted privacy.

Several things are significant about the Reinventing Government reports. First, and unlike all previous reports, they make clear that the working contexts of federal agencies restrict and inhibit the ideas, feelings, and creativity of personnel. That is to say, federal workers are not born with a "go by the book" mentality; they learn that to challenge practices or to express criticism or to articulate alternative ways of thinking is an exercise in futility. Second, the public's perception that federal workers are change-inhibiting bureaucrats reflects ignorance of and insensitivity to where these workers are coming from—that is, to gloss over this point dooms reform efforts, a conclusion that is historically confirmed.

The third significance of the reports inheres in who conceived and initiated the effort. It goes without saying that Vice President Gore is very knowledgeable about the structure and dynamics of the federal government. But so were most of those who had directed similar past efforts. I am not privy to how the vice president came to see the problem in his surprisingly refreshing way. But it is clear in the reports that he has read widely in the literature on organizations, a literature largely about business and industrial corporations. He did not need to be told that there are obvious differences between these organizations and the federal government, but he was wise enough to ask why American corporations were inefficient, noncompetitive, and going downhill rather fast for a good part of the post–World War II period? What stopped that decline? What new ideas began to be taken seriously? Were those new ideas applicable to the federal government? The overall answer is that the new ideas were not all that new except that looming disasters forced corporate executives to bite the bullet, so to speak—to be less resistant, for example, to trying to understand why Japanese companies rose from the destruction and ashes of

World War II to challenge America's economic preeminence, and in a relatively short period of time.

It is beyond my purposes and competence to attempt a comprehensive answer, but it is unassailably the case that one "new idea" was center stage. Unless workers (learners) have some meaningful role in decision making and planning, unless they feel safe to articulate their ideas and feelings, unless there is for them a realistic basis for a sense of psychological ownership, the quality of the product will suffer and production costs will be higher than they should be. You do not have to read between the lines in the Gore reports to intuit this so-called new idea, it is on the lines and is captured in the many descriptions justifying the concept of "the culture of futility." At the very least, in regard to the federal government the vice president has given currency to ideas never before articulated. That was only possible by virtue of his office and the audiences available to him. It was also possible for two other reasons: he knew the problem had been intractable, and he capitalized on personal experience in government to try to see the problem in new ways.[2]

Personal experience and the perception of intractability go a long way toward explaining why the vice president (and a supportive president) conceived the Reinventing Government initiative. *What prevents them from applying what they know to schools?* They know, as does the general public, that efforts to improve schools have generally met with little or no success. They also know from personal experience in and out of school that there is a vast difference between contexts of productive and unproductive learning, a difference so well described in the Reinventing Government reports. They do not conceptualize the difference in these terms but that is the difference they are talking about. More significant, they did not make the mistake of viewing that difference as peculiar to the

---

2.   I am not suggesting that the Reinventing Government effort is having or will have its intended effects. We do not know how it is going because there is no built-in process for evaluation and continuous improvement. I have expressed reservations about the effort, although I do not underestimate the importance of the currency of the ideas central to that report. Nor do I intend to convey the impression that most of corporate America has bought these ideas. If the time for these ideas has come, there are many who do not know it.

federal government. On the contrary, they saw kinship between the federal government and private sector organizations—that is, what they confronted in government was similar, if not identical, to what hundreds of organizational theorists and consultants have been describing for decades. It is one thing to say that the federal government is not like IBM or General Motors or AT&T; it is quite another thing to say the federal government is a unique organization sharing no similarities with them. Indeed, the Gore reports make no sense apart from one, albeit unverbalized, assumption: what happens in an organization, how well it meets its stated goals, how committed it is to self-correcting processes all depend in large part on how the capabilities, interests, outlooks of personnel are defined. Those definitions are rarely if ever put into words, but they are bedrock for comprehending the culture of an organization. It is hard to exaggerate the hold those definitions have on our thinking. You might think that when an organization—governmental, private, nonprofit, religious, educational—runs into deep trouble, those definitions would be articulated and challenged. That is seldom the case. Different diagnoses will be considered, different choices made and implemented, but those definitions go unchallenged. Nobody notices the horse is dead. Far more often than not, the diagnosis-change-implementation process is repeated, as in the case of the scores of efforts to change and improve the workings of the federal government. At some point, as in the case of the Gore reports, those definitions get challenged and new definitions come to the fore. That does not guarantee that the road ahead will be smooth but at the least it holds out the promise that the maxim "the more things change the more they remain the same" will not so easily be confirmed.

So, again, what prevents a president and vice president from applying what they apparently know about government to schools? Why in none of their public statements is there a hint of a "culture of futility" in which students and teachers are embedded? There are several reasons. One is what I shall call the unwarranted assumption of ignorance, by which I mean that having been away from schools for decades they feel that they have no basis for diagnosing the inadequacies of today's schools—that is, that schools today are not like schools in their youth; the world has changed. That the world has changed is uncontrovertible. That the basic features of schools have not changed is, in my opinion, no less incontrovertible. Kenneth Wilson, whose book *Redesigning Education* (1996) should be must reading, once said to me, "If Thomas Jefferson appeared in our midst he would find the world strange, to say the least. The one enclave he would find familiar would be schools." Cuban (1984), among others, has discussed how and why schools have not changed. Louis Gerstner, CEO of IBM, said in an op-ed piece in the *New York Times* several years ago that in the post–World War II era American business and industry had its comeuppance; it had to change "or else." Schools, he said, have not changed even though educational outcomes were depressing.

A second reason, applicable to people generally, is the inability to use personal experience. They have forgotten what they once knew: rarely were they ever turned on in a classroom; classrooms were where you did as you were told, read what you were told to read, memorized what you were told to memorize, and kept any questions you had to yourself. I use the word *told* advisedly because today, as in the past, the basic assumption is that students' minds are empty vessels that need to be filled. In the past century there have been no more than fifteen studies of question asking by students in classrooms, of which Susskind's (1969) was the most rigorous. The results of these studies are highly similar: students ask pitifully few questions, and teachers ask fantastically more questions. Before he did his study, Susskind asked teachers to estimate the number of questions they and students ordinarily ask in a forty-five-minute social studies period (students were fourth, fifth, and sixth graders in a suburban school). Teachers vastly underestimated their rate of questioning and vastly overestimated the average number of student questions. What if he had asked students to estimate? Among high school teachers I have known, a very frequent complaint is that too many students lack the motivation and interest to ask questions. "Pulling teeth" is the way one teacher put it. What is the role of student questions in learning? I have *never* met a teacher (regardless of grade level) who in any way denied that being able to ask questions was a crucial feature in facilitating productive learning.

A third reason is that when presidents and vice presidents (like people generally) think of education it is in terms of imagery of a classroom, a teacher, a school. That type of thinking is far more understandable and excusable in people generally than in political leaders who have learned that major problems are in major ways embedded in and reflect characteristics of a system. Students, teachers, classrooms are visible, palpable, directly observable; systems are not—they have to be conceptualized, their parts and relationships identified and understood. So, for example, in the Gore reports it is made clear that the inability and failure of parts of government to collaborate productively, to "cross boundaries" in ways furthering the purpose of the parts, are because of congressional restrictions. Similarly, the way the powerful Office of the Inspector General conducts itself has pervasive consequences. No one needs to tell politicians (I do not use that word pejoratively) that they operate in a system they cannot afford to ignore if they wish to survive, let alone if they wish to change it in some way. But when it comes to education, they hardly (mostly never) think in system terms. I have had opportunities to talk with elected state officials about educational reform and without exception whatever proposals they favored in no way reflected a concept of an educational system. They knew that each municipality had a school system, but their views stopped there, as if the municipal systems were not part of a larger system. I would ask, What are parts or stakeholders in the larger system and how do they affect, positively or negatively, what happens in a school? The executive and legislative branches of local and state government, the state department of education, colleges and universities who prepare educators, the federal government, parents, unions—are they not part of the system, are their influences on each other facilitative, or restrictive, or constraining, or of minor importance? No one denied all these were in the system but no one could say with assurance that they knew how the parts interacted. The imagery of the encapsulated classroom and school suffused their thinking.

In light of what I have said about political leaders in general and presidents and vice presidents in particular, what has permitted me in my recent books to conclude that unless or until the president understands the larger picture and its parts, the differences between contexts of productive and unproductive learning, the beginning steps the nation must take, the time perspective that must be adopted, educational reform is doomed? Are not those expectations unrealistic in the extreme? Am I not asking of the president an understanding that I say the president does not now have? Am I not confirming the stereotype of the professor, a retired Ivy League one at that, who indulges fantasy at the expense of reality, who confuses the marketplace of ideas with the marketplace of action? These are fair questions, which I shall endeavor to answer in subsequent chapters. At this point I wish to emphasize several things that follow from what I have said in this and the previous chapter.

What I am asking of the president—really, any person in high office—is something that *in principle* he or she already knows: when a national problem has been intractable to efforts to remedy it, the sources of the problem are many but one of them certainly is the system in which those problems arise. Another way to put it is that precisely because these have been intractable national problems one must avoid falling victim of Mencken's caveat that for every major problem there is a simple answer that is wrong. The president knows that every major problem that confronts him reflects the workings of a particular system, be it welfare, health care, foreign policy, or governmental functioning. The president does not have to be a professional educator to know that the intractability of the educational system to reform efforts says a lot about the system qua system.

Recall what happened a number of years ago when the *Challenger* spaceship containing several astronauts exploded shortly after takeoff, killing everyone on board. No one expected the president to know why it happened but we did expect that he would appoint and support investigative bodies to come up with the most probable answer. There was general agreement that the O-rings were inadequate given weather conditions on takeoff. It would have been confirmation of Mencken's caveat to conclude that the O-rings were the cause. The long and short of it is that what emerged was a system comprising different parts of the space agency and private contractors who had different and conflicting agendas, goals, concerns, and pressures. Prior to takeoff, concerns about the O-rings had surfaced but the conflicts and power plays among the parts of the system glossed over those concerns. It was an example of a tragedy waiting to be staged. It is important to note that it was some of the members on the investigative committee, notably the physicist Richard Feynmann, whose probings about the O-rings brought to the fore the inadequacies of the larger system. At least as I followed the proceedings, it seemed as if the committee from the outset assumed that the nature and inadequacies of the system had to be examined—that is, *single causes are almost never the whole story.* Systems have regulatory or governance features or processes and when something goes wrong those features cannot be ignored, because if they are, the malfunction will reappear in the same or another part of the system. The *Challenger* tragedy involved more than technical or engineering or scientific issues. These were issues in a system of parts the governance features of which were formally clear but informally tangled. The disparities between the formal and the informal were marked, as they too frequently are in complicated human systems.

It is a very different story when it comes to the educational arena. For example, one of President Reagan's earliest initiatives was to appoint a commission to come up with recommendations to deal with the falling level and quality of educational outcomes. In contrast to the starkness and immediacy of the *Challenger* tragedy, there was no one event that galvanized the president; there were many indices of unacceptable educational outcomes. If there were disputes about so-called solutions, there was none about whether there was a serious problem that was imperiling and would continue to imperil the nation's social and economic stability. The commission had the resources and freedom to define what was wrong and why. Its final report was titled *A Nation at Risk,* a document probably cited more frequently than any previous report on education. If the title of the report was intended to convey the gravity of the problem, it certainly succeeded. If the report itself was intended to clarify the complexity of the problem—that it was a congeries of problems—it was an utter failure. Glittering and high-sounding generalizations and clichés are no substitute for probing analysis, concrete description, presentation of conflicting points of view in regard to diagnosis and action, and discussion of why similar reports in the past went nowhere. Someone once said that it is hard to be completely wrong, and that is the best that can be said for this report. A more gentle but nevertheless devastating appraisal is that deep down it is shallow. But for my present purposes I wish to emphasize one feature of the report: it says absolutely nothing about the fact that not only is any given school

a complicated organization but it is embedded in a more complicated system of parts or stakeholders (local, state, and national)
not only poorly coordinated but with differing agendas, alle-
giances, and power. As with the *Challenger,* the parts of the system,
the governance features of the system, can be and have been
depicted in the form of an organizational chart—but as anyone
who has had any experience whatever in the system will attest, the
disjunction between what the organization chart depicts and what
the realities are is blatant. (That is what the Gore reports finally
and refreshingly confronted, and that is what the *Challenger* investigators knew from the outset.) The Reagan commission had tunnel vision, to the extent that it had vision at all.

There is an irony here in that President Reagan knew more, in
a limited way, than the commission. In the 1980 presidential campaign, he said that he would abolish the Department of Education.
From his perspective, one of the contributing factors to the educational mess was the intrusive, directing role of the federal government. If the distant bureaucrats were prevented from indulging
their bottomless capacity to manufacture rules and regulations, to
in effect subsidize the paper industry, the states and localities close
to where the problems are would do a far more effective and creative job. Unknowingly, the president was acknowledging that there
was a system of stakeholders, a system in which the federal government was a Johnny-come-lately. There was basically nothing
wrong with the system qua system that eliminating a federal role
would not improve. Give the responsibility back to those stakeholders closest to the problem and therefore most accountable for
how they deal with it.

This diagnosis was egregiously incomplete, and for several reasons. First, by focusing on Washington as a faulty, unwanted stakeholder, he was making the mistake the *Challenger* investigators
would have made if they had not gone beyond saying the O-rings
were *the* cause. Second, he assumed that state and local stakeholders in the system were exempt (both in the past and present) from
the criticisms he was making of the Washington stakeholders. That
assumption is patent nonsense. I do not feel compelled to judge
to what extent, if any, the Washington stakeholders made for more
noise in the system, to borrow a term from communications theory. It is sufficient for my present purpose to say that there is no

evidence whatsoever that state and local stakeholders operate (or have ever operated) in anything resembling effective or semi-effective modes of relationships. Third, he was irresponsibly ahistorical—that is, he had forgotten, if he ever knew, why and how the federal government had broken with tradition and become a stakeholder in American education. I've used the following story several times, most recently in *Revisiting the Culture of the School and the Problem of Change* (1996b), but it belongs in this discussion as well:

> A colleague of mine, Dr. Samuel Brownell, was the U.S. Commissioner of Education in the early years of the Eisenhower presidency. Dr. Brownell was quite sensitive to the dimensions of the urban problem and its increasing disorganizing and morale lowering impact on schools. It was obvious to him that neither the cities nor the states had the resources to deal with the problems, and that unless the federal government entered the picture the consequences of inaction would be socially disruptive. It was arranged for Dr. Brownell to present his case for a change in federal policy to President Eisenhower and his cabinet, a fact testifying to the significance attached to such a policy change. Dr. Brownell presented his case, following which the President asked each member of the cabinet to express an opinion. Without exception each member advised against the policy change, although some recognized the gravity of the situation. Finally, President Eisenhower turned to Vice President Nixon for his opinion and he unequivocally supported Dr. Brownell's argument and recommendations. At this point President Eisenhower expressed agreement with both Nixon and Brownell and the wheels were set in motion to develop vehicles for federal intervention [p. 92].

What Dr. Brownell was responsive to was what soon after World War II was called the *urban problem:* an insufficient tax base, insufficient and inadequate housing, racial conflict, escalating juvenile delinquency, overcrowded and physically deteriorating schools, shortages of curriculum materials, teachers, and specialized personnel, and, most clearly, a low level of quality education and educational outcomes, as well as a beginning realization of a change in the structure and functions of the nuclear family. Just as it was not the intention of Roosevelt's New Deal programs to be other than stopgap measures to get the economy over the hump, it was not the intention of the Eisenhower educational initiative to become permanent. As in the case of the New Deal programs, it soon became obvious that improving schools would not only require more money but new ideas that were in short supply in local school systems and state departments of education. Needless to say, the 1954 Supreme Court desegregation decision and the orbiting in 1957 of the Soviet sputnik each in its own way exposed an educational system unprepared to deal with the practical implications of the two events. No one was foisting government money and programs on states and localities; if anything, they were pleading for more programs and support. From the standpoint of educators in the Office of Education (later the Department of Education), if they did not prod the states and localities, using money as a carrot to stimulate interest in new programs and practices, the educational system would remain inadequate. That the federal programs were far from successful was documented early on (Berman and McLaughlin, 1978). The lack of success had many sources but one of them was the inability of both state and local government to ask this question: Was there something basically flawed in the system qua system? Could we continue with a system of governance that had hardly changed since education had been made compulsory in the nineteenth century?

I am no defender of the Department of Education. From both near and far I have come to view it as does Ravitch, who described her two-year stint there as "Adventures in Wonderland" (1995). But to claim, as President Reagan did, that eliminating the department would improve outcomes from the system reflects a degree of ignorance I consider irresponsible. To claim that the Department of Education is a spreading weed and the rest of the system is healthy green grass may satisfy the needs of ideology but nothing else.

I am sufficiently realistic not to expect that presidents and other high-level elected officials will comprehend the nature and the self-defeating features of the educational system. (I will amend that statement somewhat in the next chapter.) So why spend time criticizing them at the same time that I claim that without their leadership nothing will happen or that the situation will worsen? My answer is in several parts.

First, the fate of this society will in large part be determined by what happens in our cities and schools. If that fate is gloomy, historians of the future will render a very unfavorable verdict on the political leadership of our time for failing to be realistic, bold, and imaginative. I read a lot, I listen to talk shows, I am a fascinated viewer of C-SPAN's coverage of congressional proceedings, and I have opportunities to talk with educators and others with an interest in our cities and our schools. You have to be unusually dense or far removed from cities and their schools to avoid the conclusion that the seriousness and implications of the problems are generally recognized. Beginning with President Lyndon Johnson every president has acknowledged that conclusion. Let us not forget that the original Head Start legislation was an explicit recognition of that conclusion. And when President Carter transformed the Office of Education into a cabinet-level Department of Education, it was largely because he believed that the seriousness of the educational problems in our cities needed to be represented at the highest levels of public policy. And in their own ways Presidents Reagan, Bush, and Clinton have acknowledged that if our citics and their schools continue as they are, the stability of society is jeopardized. Today, that acknowledgment has taken a new focus: in regard to the requirements of an increasingly technological age the gulf between the students in city and suburban schools is widening quickly and dramatically and no sane person views that gulf as other than semi-catastrophic in its racial, economic, social, and vocational implications.

The point here is that precisely because it is a national problem it is obvious, and I do mean obvious, that national political leadership is required. That leadership has been exercised, with results that are, to indulge understatement, no basis for optimism.

There have been well-intentioned exercises in political leadership but there are several reasons they have been and will continue to be ineffective. First, they have not been informed by or based on the differences between contexts for productive and unproductive learning. We hear a great deal about what students should know, what skills they must acquire, but we hear next to nothing about why the culture of schools is for too many students a culture of futility. That is why Gore's Reinventing Government came as a breath of fresh air: someone at his level finally recognized that productivity in the federal government could not be understood in terms of individuals but rather in terms of a system containing incentives that were anti-productive—that is, go by the book, play it safe, keep your ideas private, roll with the punches, imagination and boldness get you nowhere, there is always retirement to look forward to. What the Gore reports describe is a context of unproductive learning. His proposals contain important features of contexts for productive learning. The most telling and instructive feature of the Gore reports is the title: *Reinventing* Government. The present system has to be changed, and radically so. It may be the case that Vice President Gore sees no kinship between the culture of futility in the federal government and the contexts of unproductive learning in American schools and classrooms. Schools and the federal government are different in many ways—but those differences in no way justify the assumption that they do not have some common characteristics (Sarason, 1996a). Schools are not literally unique organizations; they must have features in common with other organizations—if we have learned anything in this century about organizations, it is that.

A second reason presidential leadership is a necessity is that presidents know two important things. They know or have been advised that there are schools that approximate what this or that reform considers successful. I must emphasize "this or that" reform because there have been and are many and conflicting views. The other thing presidents know is that none of these reforms has spread through most, let alone all, of the system. These are important insights because they raise a crucial question: *Why haven't they spread? Why no diffusion?* There is no single answer; there never is. But there is one answer we are justified in assuming *has to be* playing a major role: *the system is not geared to spread a new idea, a new methodology, a new practice.* In fact, the more an innovation requires a noncosmetic departure from the way things are, the less likely it is to spread. The two most research-validated and reported innovations—"Success for All" (Slavin and others, 1996) and "Reading Recovery" (Clay, 1990; Pinnell, 1992; Pinnell and others, 1994)— have spread to numerous schools but the number of schools is literally a drop in the bucket when viewed in terms of the number of schools in the country. Why is this so? What is there about the system that makes spread so pitifully slow or leaves almost all of the system totally unaware of the existence of these documented reforms? No reader of this book will deny that these are crucial questions. Our last six presidents (Clinton, Bush, Reagan, Carter,

Ford, and Nixon) have not asked themselves those questions, even though in public they have proclaimed that *their* initiatives will diffuse and alter the system in the near future—that is, in five years or ten years. When President Bush put forth his Year 2000 program, he knew, his educational advisers knew, the educational community knew, and most of the public knew that it was arrant nonsense. I said that aloud and in print when the program was announced. I was then, as I am now, aghast at the number of people who thought as I did and said nothing. That says as much about cynicism as it does about the system, and in a "culture of futility" the two are different sides of the same coin, as Vice President Gore concluded about the operations of the federal government. That brings me to the third reason.

I truly do not expect presidents to make a *substantive* contribution to our educational problems. But I do expect that when a national problem has proved intractable, they will do what they are perfectly capable of doing: appoint a group of people presumably knowledgeable about the problem. I can hear readers guffawing at this suggestion—and they are justified on an actuarial basis in that the reports of most commissions, at least in the educational arena, have cornered the market on clichés, glittering generalities, pious hopes, and timidity. They are assured of a place in the dustbin of history. But I am blaming the victim because in so many of these instances, and in the educational arena it is in all instances, the president did not charge the commission with specific, concrete questions. What should we do to improve our schools? What is wrong with our schools? Those are not specific, concrete questions. They have an inkblottish character conducive to wandering all over the place. They lack the features of a helpful road map. Let me illustrate what I mean by three examples from the distant and near past.

The constitutional convention of 1787 was called to address a fact that practically no one disputed:[3] The Articles of Confederation were inadequate as a basis of forming a nation; the document

---

3.   The issue of slavery was, to say the least, a troublesome one. It became crystal clear that if clauses abolishing or containing were included, there would be no new constitution—each state would be a law unto itself, and there would be no nation. We are still paying the price of that compromise.

was not a vehicle that would protect the states and their people from foreign enemies, and it was no secure protection of individual liberties. The charge to the convention was to make specific, concrete changes for which agreement could be obtained. So, for example, if there was a need for a central government that would have increased power and responsibilities, how do you protect individual freedom from the tendency of that government to misuse power? Also, given the fact that the thirteen states would vary in geographic and population size, as well as in economic base, on what basis and how could the interests of small states be protected? The issues became increasingly specific because the answers had to be specific, spelled out. The long and short of it is that early on the convention concluded that the old system was unrescuable, and proceeded as if from scratch: Given clarity about ultimate goals, what new system was likely to achieve and sustain those goals? They did their specific task concretely and well.

The second example concerns a federal committee that began its work not long after our entry into World War II. It was created because of three very concrete facts. The war would be a long one; the number of medical-psychiatric casualties would be unprecedentedly enormous; the existing programs and resources of the Veterans Administration were inadequate in size, quality, and location (many VA hospitals were in the middle of nowhere). The issues were very specific: What kinds and numbers of specialized personnel would be required? Where would they receive training? Where should clinics and hospitals be located so as to benefit from new knowledge and practice? What incentives would be necessary for university medical centers and departments to be intimately related to and to semi-manage what would be, in comparison to before the war, galactic change in the size of the system? Here again the committee came up with what was essentially a new system; the old system was unrescuable.

The third example concerns congressional legislation for a Joint Commission on Mental Illness and Health (Joint Commission on Mental Illness and Health, 1961). Whereas the second example was for veterans, the charge here was for people in general. State programs and services for those with crippling psychological problems were utterly inadequate. State hospitals were warehouses bulging at the seams. The quality of personnel and care was poor.

There were no buffering facilities between the community and the state hospitals. States lacked both the resources and the will to build more warehouses. And, as in the case of the VA, state hospitals were removed from centers for research and improved practice. What the commission came up with was for all practical purposes a new system.

What is the relevance of these examples for dealing with the current educational system?[4] From my standpoint, in each of these examples the concept of a system informed thinking, conclusions, proposals. That concept may never (or hardly ever) have been articulated in theoretical or technical terms but it is abundantly clear that the numerous, specific problems confronting them were seen as interrelated parts of a whole, of a system. No less important, the planners knew that the fruits of their labor could not be expressed in high-sounding, hortatory generalizations but rather in a "dot the i's and cross the t's" manner. If their conclusions were, as they were expected to be, a basis for public policy and legislative action, glittering generalities had to be avoided. Also, in each example the charge to the group was both general and specific: "There is a serious problem. We cannot allow it to remain as it is. Use your experience, imagination, and creativity to give us a basis for directed action. Do not tell us to do what we have done in the past. We do not want sermons. What we need is a new vision and the concrete steps we should take to start to realize that vision. Yes, we want answers. We may not like your answers, we may disagree with this or that proposal. We expect you to tell us what to think and do. We have to act."

From time to time I indulge the fantasy that the president asks me what charge he should give to a commission to make proposals

---

4.   I decided not to include a fourth example because it did not involve a group but rather a single individual who was asked by a foundation to tell them how medical education could be improved. The foundation was the Carnegie Foundation for the Improvement of *Teaching* (italics mine). The individual was Abraham Flexner, a most eminent educator at the turn of the century. If the reader wants an example of what I mean by boldness, concreteness, system thinking, and specificity, read his *Medical Education in the United States and Canada* ([1910] 1960), a report that was used to radically alter medical education, indeed to replace one system with another. Medicine today is incomprehensible unless one understands what Flexner thought and proposed (Sarason, 1993a).

to improve the performance of our schools. Here is what I would advise the president to say:

"No one disputes that our educational system is not performing as we would like or as the future of our society requires. For more than four decades we have spent billions and billions of dollars in efforts to improve educational outcomes. The results have been very discouraging. I have been told that there have been and are isolated instances where efforts to improve schools have been successful as judged by credible research data. But I have also been told that there are no instances where the systems of which those particular schools are a part have changed. Why is it that what has been demonstrated in one school does not spread to other schools in the district, let alone to schools beyond district borders? How can you justify to a skeptical public expending money for demonstrations that, even if successful, will not be diffused generally? Is the intractability to improvement the result only of a combination of resistance to change, ignorance, apathy, or even outmoded traditional ways of thinking, or is there, in addition, something radically wrong with the system itself? That, of course, raises some very specific questions: Who are the crucial stakeholders in the system? What are the responsibilities of each? How clearly and well are they held accountable for discharging their responsibilities? If accountability is unclear and remains so, on what basis can we decide what changes to make? Does the system contain self-correcting mechanisms, and, if not, why not? What self-correcting mechanisms should we consider?

"I am not as knowledgeable about our educational system as I would like to be or must be if we are to deal effectively with the implications of an inadequate educational system for the future of our society. However, by virtue of the obligations of my office I have had to become more knowledgeable of the history of what I think is a comparable problem we have faced in the past. I refer to our military system, the many inadequacies of which were exposed during World War II. Some of those inadequacies were those of individuals but the most serious were those of a system of parts that were poorly coordinated, in hostile competition with each other, possessing no or little sense of overarching purpose, and resistant to change and innovation—a system that made accountability an intractable mystery. Significant changes were made after World War II; the situation has improved, and much more needs to be done. The point is that these changes could not have occurred without the recognition that the old system was dangerously inadequate and that noncosmetic changes were necessary. I know that systems do not change willingly, quickly, and without turmoil, which is why, I assume, we are so prone to latch onto cosmetic changes.

"If you were starting from scratch, would you come up with the educational system we now have? I am told that no knowledgeable person would answer that question in the affirmative. Is that true? If it is, I have to urge you to be as bold, candid, imaginative, serious, and concrete as possible in pointing us in new directions.

"By virtue of the responsibilities of my office I must act. I cannot, nor do I want to, appear indecisive, confused, or superficial. However, in regard to education I am far from secure about what actions to take, what vision to convey, how to decide on priorities. I am given many explanations—often mutually contradictory—for our educational ills. Let me list some of them:

- Competition among schools is virtually nonexistent. Incentives to compete and change are lacking.
- Educators are poorly prepared for the realities of classrooms, schools, and communities, especially in regard to the social-ethnic realities of our cities.
- The administrative structure and the ethos of schools and school districts are stiflingly bureaucratic, anti-change, and oppressive.
- Too many parents are distant from, uninterested in, and unsupportive of what their children learn in school and what the school expects of them.
- School personnel foster a gulf between themselves on one hand, and parents and the community on the other hand. Unless parents are given a more formal role in school policy and organization, no improvement can be expected.
- Standards for academic performance and, therefore, expectations of students have been dangerously lowered and eroded, robbing students of knowledge and skills necessary for living and working in the contemporary world. Standards should be high and taken seriously.

- Modern technology is underutilized or misutilized in aid of student motivation and learning. That is blatantly the case when one compares urban and suburban schools.
- Multiculturalism is a fact of American history and life but it is a fact poorly reflected in school curricula and in teacher-student and school-parent relationships and understandings.
- The size and organization of middle and high schools contribute to students' feeling of anonymity, lack of motivation, and boredom. Compared with life outside of school, life in school is uninteresting. In these schools student and teacher burnout is very frequent.
- The budgets of schools are too low to make achievement of their goals possible.
- It is illusory to believe that increasing school budgets will raise educational outcomes, because entrenched interests will simply throw good money after bad.
- Achievement tests, the best basis for determining whether students have learned what they are supposed to learn, have been applied in too limited a fashion, and the results have been largely ignored.
- The emphasis on achievement tests considerably narrows what we can learn and use about students' interests, talents, knowledge, and learning styles. Achievement tests tell us little about individuality. We need alternative measures that take these features into account.
- Schools should be more stringently judged by how well they prepare students for post-school living and working.
- School is not a preparation for life but life itself. The most important features of post-school living and working are features virtually absent in schools. Schools are artificial, encapsulated environments, a fact of which students are quite aware but educators and other adults are not.

"How should I judge the validity, or cogency, or importance of any of these points? Some are in the nature of an antithesis. Most, if not all of them, state a problem, but to someone like me who must act, the statements are far from instructive in regard to action. I must confess that when I review the fifteen points—and there are some I have undoubtedly overlooked—I have two reactions. The first is the feeling of being overwhelmed. That is followed by the thought that the number and gravity of the problems suggest that there is something very wrong with our educational system as a system. In saying that, I am in no way trying to impose a focus on your thinking or proposals but rather indicating that you should be unconstrained in your thinking, imagination, and boldness. Our past efforts at educational reform have been ineffective. We cannot afford to reinvent flat tires. The stakes are high, very high. Time is not on our side. As a politician and president I consider myself an expert on partisanship, the pressures of vested interests, 'one issue' thinking, and the difference and tension between doing what you think can be done and doing what *needs* to be done. I am asking you to tell me, and through me the American people, what your experience, knowledge, and inmost hearts say needs to and must be done. It may be that what you tell us will not be palatable. It may be viewed as revolutionary, too radical, too impractical. Of one thing you can be sure: the verdict of history will either commend you for your comprehension of what needs to be done or will criticize you for missing an opportunity to alert us to what needs to be done. We are not dealing with a quick-fix problem."

The first part of the charge centers specifically on the lack of diffusion and the brute fact of intractability. Those are not up-in-the-clouds issues. They are facts or issues that demand concrete explanations that point to very specific courses of action, in contrast to generalizations that point us nowhere or everywhere. (The group, of course, can conclude that it does not have the type of answers we seek and need, in which case the public will be told that in regard to action we will proceed, so to speak, by the seat of our pants and a somewhat empty head.) The second part of the charge suggests explanations of discrete problems—and these, if taken seriously, suggest that we move on all fronts as if each problem is as important as every other problem, or as if the problems are not interrelated, or as if the explanations of these problems are based on equally credible evidence. The significance of the fifteen points is that by stating them we are asking the group to assess, to pass judgment, to say that this problem is more important than that one, that this problem will have more positive percolating consequences than that one. In brief, this kind of charge would (obviously in my opinion) not produce a report that is long on rhetoric, exhortation, and sermonizing and short on everything else that might guide initial courses of action. Reports are meant to be read and understood, and by understood we ordinarily mean that we have been provided with a basis for agreeing or disagreeing with what was explicitly said about diagnosis and action. Reports should not be inkblots that are interpreted in very different ways by different people.

Leadership does not necessarily require the president to have sophisticated knowledge of a particular complex problem and its history. But it does require knowledge about how to go about getting concrete answers to these problems. Those answers may be incomplete and turn out to be in small or large part inadequate. But that inadequacy should not be a consequence of wholesale ambiguity, an avoidance of controversial conclusions, or what posterity will label as tunnel vision.

Public education today is a national problem. That is a glimpse of the obvious, of course, and it is no less obvious that whatever leadership presidents have taken has been, to be charitable, ineffective. There is and will be no substitute for that leadership. Whether the president likes it or not, or whether we like it or not, only the one in the top job can begin a national discussion that faces up to past failures and requires that we consider new alternatives that, however controversial, have to gain currency.

I am reminded here of the fanfare associated with Mr. Annenberg's gift of half a billion dollars to improve schools. In a ceremony in the Oval Office, President Clinton praised Mr. Annenberg for the gift and his recognition of the implications of the gravity of the plight of our schools, especially those in our largest metropolitan areas. It was hard for me to watch that ceremony because I had previously been an invited participant in a small meeting to advise how the money could most productively be used. It quickly became obvious to the participants that we were witnessing Scene 1 of Act 1 of another disaster in educational reform, much like the disaster of the Casey Foundation initiative (which I predicted and have discussed elsewhere; see Sarason, 1990). Everything I have since learned about how the Annenberg money is being spent confirms my worst fears. What is particularly discouraging is that President Clinton was giving his blessing and in so doing exposing his irresponsible ignorance of the fact that over the decades the federal government had spent fantastically more billions than Mr. Annenberg to achieve similar, and often identical, goals but with no discernible positive effects. Is not the pessimism (and cynicism) of the general public about school reform a reaction to that fact? What permits Mr. Annenberg and President Clinton to appear optimistic, to convey to that public that if there were many more Mr. Annenbergs, the goals of school reform will be realized? That is not leadership, it is do-goodism, excusable in a Mr. Annenberg but not in a president.

What constitutes political leadership? In the next chapter let us go back to Thomas Jefferson and his era.

Chapter Three

America's Only Serious Education President

The word *education* does not appear in the Constitution. Indeed, from all that was written at the time about the shaping of a new nation, one might conclude that there was no interest in why, where, how, and by whom youth should be educated. There were two major reasons for the omission. The first was that it was a matter of *obvious* principle—political, moral, and pedagogical—that education was a responsibility of family and community. It was not a responsibility of a central government far removed from the sites of education. The framers of the Constitution had no need to articulate the strong belief that only those who obviously were the most direct stakeholders in formal education should decide what that education should be. It was literally inconceivable that it should be otherwise. Besides, it was axiomatic that centralized government and authority were evils, albeit necessary ones, which had to be constrained and prevented from increasing in power, and—as history documented—any increase in government's assigned powers was a threat to individual freedom. I think it is fair to say that if the leaders of the time were to observe today's educational scene they would be aghast at the degree to which the substance and process of formal learning is determined by individuals and groups (near and far) who have no direct, concrete knowledge of and no personal, intimate relationship to the context of learning. We, today, could try to explain to them how this change came about, but our explanation would be unconvincing because to them the history would be about a step-by-step departure from the principle that in matters educational only those with the most direct, personal responsibility for children should determine what goes on, why, and for which purposes. And to them that meant parents and the small, local community.

The second reason, related to the first, was no less obvious: the purpose of education was to give youth the tools to become free individuals who would live in and protect a free society. That was not empty rhetoric. The framers of the Constitution saw themselves and their fledgling nation in a world containing enemies, internal and external, and to withstand those threats required a citizenry educated to understand the nature and history of tyranny. The Bill of Rights was to be taken seriously: individuals were encouraged and expected to speak their minds, however controversial and idiosyncratic their spoken or written words. In his first inaugural address, Jefferson said, "If there be any among us who would wish to destroy this union or to change its republican form, let them stand undisturbed as monuments of the safety with which error of opinion can be tolerated where reason is left free to combat it." And it was Jefferson who near the end of his life articulated what Commager (1975, p. 5) called "the animating principle of Jefferson's age": "We believed that man was a rational animal. . . . We believed that men, habituated to thinking for themselves, and to follow reason as guide, would be more easily and safely governed than with minds nourished in error and debased by ignorance." The earlier Pilgrims and Puritans saw learning to read as absolutely essential for comprehending and defending biblical teachings. Satan was the enemy of God's ways. That conception of the overarching purpose of education had changed markedly by the time the colonies became the United States of America, as Commager beautifully summarizes:

> [There was] no need to campaign for the secularization of education. It was, by Old World standards, already secularized. One of the purposes of creating public schools in the Bay Colony was to outwit "ye ould deluder Satan," but that maneuver was directed by the secular branch of the community, not the ecclesiastical, or— if it was difficult to make this distinction in the 1640s—that was certainly true during the era of the Enlightenment. No religious tests sifted applicants to colleges and universities (not until 1871

could dissenters attend the universities of Oxford or Cambridge), nor were there religious tests for professors. In the seventeenth century a Baptist sat in the president's chair at Harvard College, and in the opening days of the nineteenth century a Unitarian was elected to the Hollis Chair of Divinity (As late as 1862, Cambridge University turned down a professorship of American history on the ground that the incumbent might be a Unitarian!). The charter of the College of Rhode Island, established especially for the proper training of Baptists, provided that "all members shall forever enjoy free, absolute, and uninterrupted liberty of conscience" and that the board of trustees should include Anglicans, Congregationalists, and Quakers. So, too, trustees of the new College of Philadelphia included Presbyterians and Anglicans, as well as Quakers, and Franklin, who was a deist, served as the first president of the board. Jefferson's new University of Virginia was based on "the illimitable freedom of the human mind." "Here," he wrote, "we are not afraid to follow truth wherever it may lead, nor to tolerate any error as long as reason is left free to combat it" [1975, p. 15].

The thrust of these introductory comments is that in Jefferson's era leaders understood the difference between education and indoctrination, between encouraging curiosity and stifling it, between the freedom to express and the fear to express, between a marketplace of ideas and one with nothing or little to sell or buy. They were not, I should hasten to add, educational theorists who developed a pedagogy consistent with their conceptions of the needs, minds, capabilities, and ambitions of *American* citizens, and I italicize American for the simple reason that no one was in doubt (including foreign observers) that the new country's people were and should be a breed apart. In brief, it would be quite misleading to attribute to these early political leaders a sophistication about the relation between educational theory and practice they did not have. But it is not wrong to say that they had an extraordinarily clear conception of the overarching purpose of education: to nurture and sustain independence of thinking, expression, and action. To be sure, there were other purposes—but none as important as independence of view and expression, without which European class-political-economic inequities and tyrannies would transfer to these shores. When these political leaders spoke of freedom, it was because of the reality and immediacy of threats to that freedom.

There was another point that these early leaders, and people generally, considered so obvious that it did not have to be made explicit. Education took place in more than formal sites of learning. From an early age children were expected to assume household responsibilities, a kind of division of labor, ranging from cooking, sewing, repairing to the care of siblings. In what was primarily an agrarian society those responsibilities were many, varied, and crucial. Children were not only expected to perform these tasks, they wanted to. The legendary one-room school was prototypical in this respect in that each school contained children varying in age and ability (and probably interest) and older children had to be given some responsibility for teaching or supervising or caring for younger children. One teacher in one such classroom had to devise some degree of division of labor. The important point is that the worlds in and out of school were not as psychologically and intellectually separated or divorced from each other as they later became. That, of course, was not a matter of any educational theory or pedagogical practice. It was a matter of necessity and a conception of what children could and should learn and do; and these two matters were taken seriously. If the political leaders did not have or articulate the relations between a theory of productive learning and pedagogical practice, they were very familiar with Rousseau's theory of learning and its political and developmental implications. If Rousseau was clear about anything, it was the importance of exquisite sensitivity to a child's interests and curiosities, which were the starting points of a process for awakening, broadening, and deepening the child's capabilities, skills, and knowledge. Rousseau's writings played a significant role in the events and thinking that culminated in the French Revolution of 1789, a fact of which American leaders were quite and approvingly aware. If we cannot truly say that American leaders consciously and deliberately sought to apply Rousseau's theory to formal schooling, we can say that they viewed children as precious, multifaceted resources whom it was the duty of a free society to nurture and support in ways that would produce free individuals, not individuals who would be required to conform blindly to unexamined doctrine. When you read the observations and conclusions of foreign observers who came to these shores in those early days, they express surprise at how individuals of differing ages, status, and economic level gave voice to opinion, thought, and criticism. Obeisance to long-standing tradition and practice was notable by its absence. It was the duty of one generation of free people to reproduce the next generation of free people. The concept of freedom cannot be defined in brief, simple terms. But in the late eighteenth and early nineteenth centuries one of the most obvious features of the concept exemplified in quotidian living was the obligation to give expression to what one thought and felt, and it was the obligation of everyone to respect expression of the thought, opinion, and feelings of others.

I am not trying to convey a picture of an early utopia where everything was sweetness and light and harmony reigned. It was not a Garden of Eden, although the early settlers so described the new continent. But it was a time and place where there was an unexcelled awareness that freedom should suffuse all areas of individual and institutional existence. That awareness was matched by boldness and a degree of consistency unmatched in history. I cannot refrain quoting from Commager's lecture on an occasion celebrating the upcoming 1976 Bicentennial:

> What happened to that deep sense of obligation to the past that animated most of the Founding Fathers, the obligation to preserve the heritage of civilization from Judea and Greece and Rome and, in the political and constitutional arena, from the Mother Country—a commitment which linked the new nation, even as she was embarking upon the boldest of experiments, irrevocably to the Old World, so that the most innovative of revolutions was also the most conservative? What happened to the deep and passionate sense of fiduciary obligation to posterity which animated all the Founding Fathers and admonished them to pass on their heritage intact to their descendants, even "to the thousandth and thousandth generation"? What happened to that devotion to the commonwealth which animated a Franklin, an Adams, a Jefferson, a Washington, a Mason, a Madison, a Wilson to wear out their lives, and their fortunes, too, in the public service, and which gave us, in a single generation, a galaxy of public leaders we have never been able remotely to duplicate since then? What happened to that ingenuity, that resourcefulness, that creativity which fashioned, again in a single generation, all those great political institutions on whose capital we have been living ever since? What happened

to that confidence in Reason, and in the ability of men to solve
their most formidable problems by the application of Reason;
to that confidence in the ultimate common sense and even wisdom
of the people—a confidence which was at the basis of the passion
for freedom of the human mind in every area, religion, politics,
science, and morals?

When we have answered these questions we may perhaps
set about restoring the intellectual and moral world which the
Enlightenment created, and which we have lost or betrayed. That
is the most important item on the agenda of the Bicentennial
years [1975, p. xix].

As Commager frequently notes, slavery was a glaring, mocking
exception to the "passion for freedom." Ironically, there was one
aspect of slavery that emphasized how people understood (too
weak a word) the indissoluble connection between education and
freedom: the Southern states made it illegal to educate blacks. If
slaves were taught to read and write, if they were exposed to the
history of the struggle for freedom, they would get the "wrong
ideas," the very ideas that powered the American "white" revolution. These Southern states were paying tribute to the overarching
purpose of education at the same time they denied that education
to blacks. They correctly knew that education that was not deliberate indoctrination was dangerous precisely because it opened up
vistas on what the human mind could be, create, and accomplish.
They knew that indoctrination was not education as they understood it. As Commager says, the passion for freedom had to put its
stamp "in every area, religion, politics, science, and morals." As we
shall now see, and as Commager's essays make plain, "in every
area" included education. That, in those earlier times, was a
glimpse of the obvious. Today it is not. The modal American classroom, public or private, secular or religious, has more of the features of indoctrination than of a passion for freedom. More of this
later.

Let me now list Jefferson's accomplishments and leadership in
the educational arena. He castigated the European tradition of two
types of education: that for "gentlemen of the elite" and that for
"the rabble." Even a fervent libertarian like Voltaire looked upon
education for the lower classes as, at best, semi-wasteful. Jefferson,

like many of his cohorts, pronounced anathema on such a view and practice even though he was part of an American elite. For Jefferson, the democratization of education required that it go beyond the elementary school into higher education.

In 1779, he proposed to the Virginia legislative a three-part plan: a system of elementary schools feeding into grammar schools, and then into the university. He also proposed that the very low quality of the College of William and Mary be radically reformed, including new chairs of law, medicine, and modern languages. He considered it essential to establish a state library. In 1816, he proposed a more ambitious plan that included what Commager (1975, p. 69) described as "the astonishing provision of a literacy test for citizenship."

The creation of the University of Virginia was Jefferson's doing. He was chairman of the Board of Trustees. He was the first rector of the university, and indeed he designed every building, every column, every window, every door, and every mantelpiece. He planted every tree, shrub, and flower, laid out every path, and built every wall. He provided the library, chose the professors and students. He drew up the curriculum and dedicated the university "to the illimitable freedom of the human mind."

As Commager delightfully comments, "Not bad that for a man in his eighties." The university was at its birth not only the most eminent in the United States, as Jefferson said, but the most enlightened and the most liberal, the most nearly like some of the great universities in the Old World. And it was also Jefferson who was chairman of the committee that drafted the Land Ordinance of 1785 containing provisions establishing the policy of setting aside public lands for the support of schools and universities, a policy that was later extended to all newly acquired territories.

Bear in mind that throughout his life Jefferson was formally or informally a major figure on the American scene. If the descriptive label workaholic had been in currency at that time, it could have been legitimately applied to him. I say that only semi-facetiously to make the point that one of the tests of great political leadership is the courage, strength, and persistence with which a leader pursues an issue he or she regards as essential for the public welfare, even though that issue may arouse resistance and controversy. Not all of Jefferson's proposals met ready acceptance. Not everyone considered education as important as he did, although they considered it important. No other leader at the time immersed himself as he did in the details of the organization of an educational *system*. No one articulated more or as well as he that the overarching purpose of education was to free, not indoctrinate, minds, to produce questioners and not narrow or mindless conformists, to inculcate the morality undergirding freedom, not a morality that closed minds to new or alternative ideas. And Jefferson was never in doubt that what he wanted for people was what people wanted for themselves and what alone would prevent the new nation from regressing to the class distinctions of the Old World.

Jefferson had standards of quality. He was interested in far more than building schools, universities, and libraries. He wanted teachers capable of stimulating minds. He was most clear on that in regard to universities. So, for example, he did not succeed in reforming the College of William and Mary, one means for which was his proposal to bring over the faculty of the University of Geneva, one of the most respected European Universities! He sought quality wherever or in whomever it was. Education was too important for the individual and nation to be entrusted to pedestrian minds.

In previous chapters I very briefly distinguished between contexts of productive and unproductive learning. Although Jefferson said little about those distinctions, I have no doubt that he would have considered that distinction a glimpse of the obvious. Commager correctly notes that unlike Rousseau or Pestalozzi or Grundtvig, Jefferson was not an original educational thinker, he was "with Lord Brougham and Wilhelm von Humboldt, the greatest educational statesman of his day" (p. 70). There are two considerations—one more speculative than the other—which in my opinion suggest that Jefferson was more than a statesman, that he well understood some of the most important features of contexts of productive learning. I am not trying to make more of Jefferson than he was: I am going to suggest that certain things were so obvious to him that he had no need to articulate a pedagogy for productive learning.

I do not think it is unwarranted speculation to suggest that he assumed—one of those "of course" assumptions that did not require articulation—that the people of the new, small nation wanted and hungered for education for their children, and that that hunger would be transmitted to them. He could count on that. Today it is hard for us to grasp how concerned those people were about the fragility of the new nation in its efforts to survive, confronted as it was with enemies and a paucity of those human resources required for nation building. National pride required an educated citizenry. That message required no hard sell to the adult citizens and neither did parents have to sell it to their children. What I am suggesting is that Jefferson did not have to articulate that wanting was crucial for productive learning. That articulation was necessary by educational theorists in a class-based Europe whose ruling, nondemocratic elites viewed education of *all* of its masses as dangerous and wasteful; maintaining the status quo was their aim. Why educate people who could not assimilate or benefit from education? To Jefferson and everyone else in the new nation, that question was politically and morally sinful.

There was another "of course" in Jefferson's outlook on education and that was that the schoolhouse would be a small place with, by our standard today, a very small number of children. The one-room school was the norm. Jefferson never looked favorably on the possibility that America would be other than a predominantly agricultural nation. He looked upon Europe's large, crowded, and conflict-ridden dominating cities as something the new nation would and should not foster. This was a comparatively large country. It became much larger as a result of actions Jefferson took during his presidency. Nevertheless, he wanted a country whose institutions and communities were small and literally connected to the land, not divorced from it. So when he envisioned a school, it was the polar opposite of what schools ultimately became. However imaginative a mind Jefferson had, he could not imagine the size of our schools today. If he never articulated a theory of learning and pedagogy, everything we know about him permits the conclusion that he would have regarded the size of today's classrooms and schools as patently inimical to productive learning. He would have readily agreed that a context of productive learning requires a degree and quality of teacher-child relationships possible only in a small group. Jefferson increased the size of the country—but not for the purpose of increasing the size of communities and the institutions they needed and for which they were responsible. Jefferson would have applauded the saying "small is beautiful."

Now for the second and more speculative reason. Jefferson was, among many other things, a writer. Practically all that he wrote was deeply personal, concerned as those writings were with hopes, fears, issues, all very strongly felt. He wrote about the world as it had been, was, and should be in the future. Nowhere was this more true than when he wrote about education. My speculation—which I really do not regard as such—has two facets. The first is that Jefferson knew and appreciated that *he* had had opportunities, stimulation, and resources (for example, books and teachers) that vastly enlarged and enriched his understanding of himself, others, and his world. It is to indulge understatement to say that he was an introspective and reflective person. When he wrote, he drew upon personal experience. All writers do that, however marked, indirect, or unacknowledged the expression of that experience may be. When Jefferson wrote about education, his statements were informed by personal imagery from myriads of sources. The second aspect is that Jefferson wanted his and future generations of young people to have the educational opportunities he had and that meant a quality and context of learning that would be the opposite of indoctrination, of knowledge divorced from personal significance or practical and social applications, of instruction that would not sustain the distinctive human attribute to want to know and explore.

Jefferson did not write about a pedagogy for the classroom. Pedagogy is more than how to teach, or techniques or approaches geared to obtaining stated objectives. Pedagogy is the overt expression of the relationships among a theory of the learning process, conceptions of the needs and abilities of learners, and strategies that reflect the theory and conceptions. Pedagogy is a form of the self-fulfilling prophecy. That is to say, if you start with theory X, conception Y, and strategy Z, you expect to achieve the desired objective; that is the way you set it up. You may know there are other X's, Y's, and Z's, but you eschew them because you regard them as inappropriate, inadequate or harmful in some way, unnecessary, or downright wrong. How should one decide between different pedagogies? That question is in principle identical to asking how we should decide between different forms of government—

for example, democratic or authoritarian. If you believe that people are both interested in and capable of participating in the political process, that they want to be heard and their opinions respected, that forums should exist where opposing ideas are articulated—if your thinking goes in that direction you will opt for one form of government. If you believe that people need to be directed and instructed, that they do not know what is good for them, that they need to be firmly led and controlled, that if you give them an inch they will demand a mile because they cannot tell the difference between freedom and license—if you think in these ways authoritarian government will appeal to you. The two forms of government lead to very different pedagogies.

It is no different in the case of classroom pedagogy. How would Jefferson have judged today's modal classroom and school as he learned that as students traversed the grades the strength of wanting to learn, to be motivated and interested, decreased; that students were passive, nonquestioning learners; that the gulf between life in school and life outside of it was enormous to the point of unbridgeability; and that despite these facts the existing pedagogy continued to be employed and justified? To a Thomas Jefferson whose devotion to and clarity about freeing the mind from any source of restriction and constriction, the modal classroom would be a disaster.

Thomas Jefferson was not an educational theorist and he did not leave us an explicit pedagogy. He was a political and educational statesman who throughout his long life in public office and service saw the connections between a freeing education and a free society. That is why, despite his countless obligations and responsibilities, he considered his achievements in the educational arena as among the most important. He not only wrote about education, he acted in very concrete ways. If he had done aught but leave us with inspiring generalizations about a free people in a free society, history would have regarded him favorably. If he said that the pressures of time and office limited his contributions to education to generalizations, we today would say we understand. But that is my point: he understood very well that generalizations were not enough, that actions at *all* levels of education were required. He did not create the University of Virginia as an exercise in the aesthetics of architecture but as a place in which faculty and students would interact and intellectually struggle with the most important problems of history and the day.

In Jefferson's day the problem was creating sites and gaining fiscal support for education for *all* young people at *all* levels of education. Improving education was far less a problem than making education possible. Today our task is to improve education. There is complete agreement that that is our responsibility. About how to discharge that responsibility there is nothing resembling agreement either within the educational community or among public officials. In the first presidential debate in the 1996 campaign both Senator Dole and President Clinton emphasized their total commitment to improving schools. In an hour-and-a-half debate, between fifteen and twenty minutes were devoted to a give-and-take under two headings: the Department of Education and school choice. (In addition to that give-and-take each candidate referred to education many times.) Senator Dole advocated the elimination of the Department of Education and advocated for school choice. President Clinton was for school choice; he was not opposed to vouchers that would use private funds to send students to private schools, and he favored the creation of several thousand schools "created by teachers and parents, sometimes by businesspeople, called charter schools, that have no rules."

Jefferson was our first and last serious education president, by which I mean that he was clear, knowledgeable, and *inquiring* about the means and purposes of learning, and what some European educational theorists had written. And when one reads about the many roles he played in creating the University of Virginia, to say that he was an active educator is an understatement. By contrast, Senator Dole and President Clinton come off as rank, uninformed, well-intentioned amateurs who for all practical purposes are not interested in becoming knowledgeable. Their working knowledge of schools and school systems appears to be virtually nil. Let me explain that statement by analogy. During the Cold War a president had to develop, or change, or take action in regard to the then Soviet Union. Being personally unfamiliar with the Soviet Union he had to depend on what he had read on his own and what different parts of the executive branch provided him, most notably the State Department, the Joint Chiefs of Staff, the CIA, and the National Security Council. He not only had to read a great deal, he frequently met with representatives from these agencies. What he read and discussed concerned many things but they all focused on such questions as: What are we dealing with? What changes, if any, have occurred in power relationships among the ruling elite? What is the health of the Soviet economy? Have any changes occurred in Soviet foreign policy? There were many more questions for each of which there were data varying from hard to soft, from clear to ambiguous in significance, from relevant to tangential to this or that particular issue, from sheer speculation to educated guesses. And all of this in varying degrees placed in the context of Soviet history and our relationship to it. Precisely because the Soviet Union was a totalitarian society, Kremlinology became a specialized field of study, one aspect of which was intuiting the Soviet mind-set. The point is that the president did not have to be convinced that he had to be knowledgeable about all facets of our relationships with the Soviet Union. No convincing was necessary; he knew the problems were too important to allow him to be simply a passive recipient of data and opinion. I have no doubt that the president spent a significant fraction of his time reading, talking, and thinking about the Soviet Union.

I have no doubt that by comparison the president spends an insignificant fraction of his time on public education; that he feels far less compelled (if compelled at all) to become knowledgeable about the history and complexity of educational problems. Looking back to the Cold War, it seems clear that to the president of the time, the Soviet Union was far more "sexy" a problem than American education. After all, one could ask, was not the Soviet Union a clear, immediate threat to our leadership of the free world and to our national security? Of course it was. It needs to be noted, however, that there was one assumption on which our policies and actions in regard to the Soviet Union was based: the Soviet Union would remain the familiar Soviet Union we had known. No one in government was prepared for the speed with which the Soviet Union crumbled and disintegrated, which is another way of saying that available data, their interpretation, and opinion about the Soviet Union had been grievously misleading or wrong. What we have been learning since the demise of the Soviet Union is that there were people there who years before its demise had already concluded that it could not continue as it had. And, as we now know, their beginning efforts to change the society unleashed forces that could not be controlled. The system was unrescuable.

It is ironic that in that first 1996 campaign debate it went unnoticed that despite sharp surface differences between the candidates they were in implicit agreement about one point radical in its implications for what each was proposing, a point that if not taken seriously could negatively transform the society. More correctly, it could continue to transform the society; the transformation has been going on for decades but, as in the case of the Soviet Union, its dynamic nature has not been recognized. The point of unrecognized agreement was that the current educational system is grossly flawed and we must seek ways to bypass it—for example, through vouchers, schools "without rules" and not part of a school system, and lessening and disempowering educational bureaucracies. Those and other similar proposals—by the candidates and many other people—can only be offered on the assumption that the system as it is is incapable of achieving desired outcomes. But neither candidate could draw that conclusion, let alone contemplate or discuss it. Just as presidents assumed that with all its weaknesses and inefficiencies the Soviet Union would be with us in the foreseeable future and beyond, the candidates assumed that our educational system is basically rescuable if we apply the right kinds of Band-Aids or if by demonstrations of a few thousand new, unencumbered schools, the thousands of encumbered schools will change their ways.

Although I believe the system is not rescuable, I do not expect others to agree with me. After all, it took me decades to come to that belief and I had to overcome a lot of internal resistance even to verbalize it. But I am not asking for agreement. I am asking that it be discussed because it speaks to the vague feelings of many, many people that the future is gloomy. In regard to our urban schools those feelings are not inchoate. Those school systems are written off as hopeless, even though people who hold that view agree that what happens in urban schools will adversely affect our society. And yet neither candidate said anything about urban schools except in the most indirect and allusive ways.

What do I mean when I say that I expect a president to be knowledgeable about education? The simple way of answering the question is to say that I expect him or her, like Thomas Jefferson, to be as interested in the many facets of classrooms, schools, and school systems as in foreign policy, agriculture, commerce, the environment, and the like. The president should be knowledgeable enough to realize that there are some questions that require confrontation and that must be answered:

- Why is it that despite the scores of billions of dollars spent on education in the post–World War II era, there is little to show for it?
- Why is it that as students go from elementary to middle to high school, their interest in and motivation for learning decreases?
- Why is it that when there is credible evidence that a particular school context in a particular school system achieves desirable outcomes—in some cases where those outcomes exceed previous expectations—that demonstration does not spread elsewhere in the school system or beyond?
- Why is it that when people are asked that if they were given the opportunity to start from scratch and create a school system, they do not say they would create the system we now have?

I am not asking a lot of a president whose most minimal knowledge about education must indicate that the situation is too serious, too fraught with adverse consequences for the society, to justify inaction or proposing programs that are retreads from the past. I am not asking the president to be able, initially at least, to answer these questions in any depth. The president has many ways of getting answers to these questions. The questions will generate a variety of answers; that is clear ahead of time. But unlike past presidents he or she will be posing some very concrete questions, in contrast to asking open-ended questions of such generality or vagueness as to get answers that wander all over the lot and more often than not are hortatory, empty rhetoric. There is a vast difference between a president who passively asks others how and what he or she should think about, and a president who asks: "Here are some troubling, puzzling questions to which I would like some very detailed answers so that I have a basis for deciding what I must do, how I should lead."

Before he became president, John Kennedy was a member of the Congress that established the Joint Commission on Mental Illness and Health. He, like many others, knew three things: mental health was a serious national problem; the state hospital system was glaringly, immorally inadequate; and the disjunction between the number of people who required help and the number of relevant professionals was very great. Crucially, his interest in mental health issues was personal in that one of his siblings required sustained hospitalization. The commission issued its report in 1961, although its substance was known before publication. In 1963, in his address to Congress, President Kennedy presented proposals that went beyond the commission's report and had the effect of radically transforming the mental health system—for example, giving it a community-based orientation in addition to emphasizing the promotion of health, of wellness, and prevention as coequal in importance with the repair orientation. That was an instance of a president who for personal, societal, and political reasons had become knowledgeable about a major problem that compelled him to exercise bold leadership.

My comments about education and presidential leadership were not for the purpose of saying that the president should act. Indeed, I would argue that at the present time any action is likely to be as fruitless as past actions. What is required is presidential action that will give us a far more secure basis for answering the four questions I posed earlier. Those answers will be provisional; there will be no unanimity; they will vary in imaginativeness and boldness; they will (or should) stimulate debate and controversy about relatively concrete questions, not questions that have the characteristics of inkblots. And that debate and controversy cannot take place absent political, presidential leadership.

I am of the opinion that one of the four questions is the most crucial. I refer to the fact that there have been many isolated examples—the "heres and the theres" many of which never get published—of classrooms and schools that changed from unproductive to productive contexts of learning. As luck sometimes has it, I began to write these words on the day (October 20, 1996) that an article appeared in the Connecticut section of the *New York Times*. The article is by a reporter, Fred Musante, who—among other things—sought and attained his teaching credentials. The article is about New Haven's High School in the Community (HSC), an alternative high school created in 1970, a time when social unrest in the city was on the front pages of major newspapers around the country. The Black Panther-Bobby Seale trial was in progress, the National Guard was called out, most people had a siege mentality, racial conflict in the schools was a daily occurrence. A handful of teachers sought permission to create their own small high school. Trickett's 1991 book describes in detail how the school was created, its unusual governance and structure, and its accomplishments. It is important to note that permission was not enthusiastically granted; the powers that be were desperate, anything that would or could be a place for troubling and troubled minority students (and some vocal, militant teachers) should be tried if only to prevent escalation of criticism of the city's school. Musante summarizes aspects of the story well:

> In 1967, Hillhouse High School erupted in racial violence, explained Matt Bornstein, High School in the Community's math teacher, computer coordinator and unofficial historian. Some of Hillhouse's teachers were upset at their school administration's solution to the riots, which was to cut short the school day to keep opposing white and black students separated. "That is still a problem in our society," he observed.
>
> He, Ms. Wolf and some other teachers felt another approach would be better, and in 1970 they opened their "high school without walls" with 150 students in a former auto parts store. The following year, a second unit started in space in a girdle factory. They were later combined in a community hall of a public housing project.
>
> When its Federal grants ran out, High School in the Community settled into an abandoned elementary school built in 1888, where it stayed for 20 years. The building was decrepit, but with poverty came the freedom to experiment. . . .
>
> Most of all, the hallmark of its educational philosophy was a democratic organization. As close as possible students are admitted to maintain a balance of one third each white, black and Hispanic, half male and half female, but otherwise by lottery with no advantage for higher levels of ability. As a result, the school is

not a collection of angels or geniuses like some other magnet
schools that "skim the cream."

HSC has no principal!

Several years after the school opened I met semi-weekly over a
year with the teachers of the school, far less for whatever help I
could be than because I wanted to check out what friends and Yale
colleagues (Edison Trickett, Edward Pauly, Willis Hawley) connected with the school had been telling me. They were for me
inspiring meetings. They were especially instructive (and discouraging) in regard to the countless obstacles encountered in dealing
with the system.

What lessons did the system draw from HSC? How did that system seek to spread the significance of HSC to other parts of the
system? It is true that one of the creators of HSC years later started
a somewhat comparable high school. But it is also true that, these
two schools aside, New Haven's schools have been influenced not
at all. I consider that failure to spread to speak volumes about why
the educational reform movement has had no generalizing effects.

But there is another reason why the lack of spread of a HSC
and other "heres and theres" is so important to confront: we have
learned a lot about the differences between contexts of productive
and unproductive learning. We are not babes in the woods in these
matters. That is not to say we know all we need to know. But we
know enough to conclude that unless we seriously confront and
comprehend the system's failure to spread what we do know, what
has been demonstrated, the inadequacies of our schools will continue—or, more likely, get worse.

The lack of spread aside, diverse answers to the other questions
have been put forth. Some of them have their kernels of truth—
but the proposals derived from those kernels have been far from
encouraging, let alone widespread. The significance of the spread
question is that it forces one to come to grips with the system qua
system, not only with classrooms, or individual schools, or school
districts but with all the different stakeholders in our educational
system, including state departments of education, parents, legislatures, executive branches, colleges and universities, and unions.
The lack of spread is quintessentially, blatantly, a symptom of system

malfunction. Up until now reform efforts have dealt with this or that part—really parts of parts—as if the system in which those parts are embedded does not present mammoth obstacles or does not support attitudes, practices, and purposes inimical to reform.

An analogy may be helpful here. One of Freud's contributions was his emphasis on the complex, subtle, and unintended ways individual symptomatology arises and is supported by family dynamics—that is, the family drama. Despite that emphasis he developed an individual psychoanalytic therapy that mightily influenced almost all other approaches to helping individuals. The results were and are far from robust. It took decades after Freud for some therapists to ask: If neurotic symptoms of an individual arise and are maintained in the context of the family, should we not deal with the family as a family, as a system of interacting individuals, rather than dealing only or primarily with the individual? That question led to the development of family therapy, which in the case of children is more economical and effective than prolonged therapy with the individual child. In brief, once the fact that the family is a social system was taken seriously, the technical problem was one of how to deal with and alter that system in appropriate ways.

We have not taken the concept of system seriously in regard to education. A recent, notable, and stimulating exception is Kenneth Wilson's *Redesigning Education* (1996), in which he clearly emphasizes the significance of the lack of spread of deserving innovations. And his emphasis is powered by many examples outside the field of education that illuminate how far we are from thinking about education in system terms. I do not consider it happenstance that Wilson came to education from a field in which the concept of system is second nature to its members. Wilson is a physicist, a world-class one. There are other hard scientists who got interested in education but who did not at all take seriously or apply the concepts of system so fundamental in their previous work; their contributions to education have been minor or nil—or have added to the confusion. Wilson is an exception.

The immediate task is not how to answer the question but how to give it currency. And by currency I mean alerting the general public to the importance of the question and to the real possibility that when answers are forthcoming, they may require changes that will be unfamiliar, controversial, and critical of current stake-holders, who understandably will not respond enthusiastically. To expect an unprepared public to respond with serious interest to such answers is to make the most frequent mistake of reformers: to spring a proposal or program before those who will be affected by it have had time to think about it, to digest it.

To give currency to the questions I posed can come about in different ways but none is as influential as presidential-political leadership, with its power to investigate heretofore intractable problems. I can, as I have, written about these questions. Wilson has and will continue to do the same.[1] Our audiences are minuscule. The point is not whether Wilson or I have come up with answers but rather that the questions have not been brought to the attention of the general public. What is at stake here is no piddling matter. What is at stake is the future of the society. In such matters the presidential role is primarily moral and educational—that is, to become knowledgeable, to seek answers in diverse ways, and to present the issues concretely, clearly, and frequently. We know all too well that presidents are politicians used to compromise and very able to speak out of both sides of the mouth. But, as I have emphasized, I am not asking the president for answers but rather for action to launch a commission charged with the task of providing relatively concrete answers to relatively concrete questions. Although its members will not be asked to cover the waterfront, they will be unable to avoid coming to grips with the system as a system and seeing its familiar parts in an unfamiliar way.

Jefferson knew well that posterity is the cruelest of critics, that it would judge him, other political leaders, and the new nation not for their idealistic philosophy of freedom and democracy but for the courage, wisdom, and persistence of actions to implement and protect those ideals. He had an eye on posterity in regard to all that he proposed and did. Today and in the recent past it is

---

1.   John Goodlad's books of recent years are very much on the mark and I urge the reader to give them serious study. Unlike Wilson or me, Goodlad has throughout his long career held important roles in educational settings; for example, he was long dean of the School of Education at UCLA. His most recent book, *In Praise of Education* (1997), is a good place to start and it contains references to his previous writings.

unfortunately fair to say that in regard to matters educational our presidents and political leaders generally have been content to do what they think *can be done* and remain oblivious to what *needs to be done,* even though, as posterity will undoubtedly note, what they did plainly was of no avail. If I believe that, it has been and will be no reason for me to stop saying what I say (repetitively?) in this and previous books. The stakes are too high.

Chapter Four

Test Scores: Sources of Confusion

In this chapter I turn to an issue concerning educational outcomes for which presidents and people generally have no doubt about what constitutes the most important criterion of success: performance on achievement tests. If that is true for the general public, it is in part because our recent presidents (and governors and others whose pronouncements are reported in the mass media) have proclaimed that if their initiatives are adopted, tests scores would rise and exceed or compare favorably with other industrialized nations. Indeed, these presidents have supported legislation for national standards and assessment—a kind of score card—that would enable us to judge whether we are winning or losing the game of preparing our youth adequately for productive lives. Thus national assessment is viewed no differently than measures of Gross National Product—if that economic measure increases each year we are in good shape, if it stays the same or decreases, we may be in real trouble. That is why in the 1960s, when test scores began to decline, national anxiety began to increase steadily, and that is why today when test scores remain the same or increase slightly there is relief that the situation is looking up.

Imagine a day when our newspaper front pages or our TV screens inform us that achievement test scores have finally and dramatically met high standards of performance. Does anyone doubt that the president or others in high public office would tell us that our educational system was doing the job we had long hoped it would do? Needless to say, for reasons I have given in earlier chapters and will give in this and later ones, that imagined day will not come as long as we continue present policies and the thinking undergirding them. When I imagine that day, as I frequently do, it elicits this question: How would Thomas Jefferson have greeted those desirably elevated test scores? I, at least, have no doubt that he would be both puzzled and perturbed. What, he would ask, do those scores tell us about minds that are free and independent? Jefferson was an avid collector of statistics, and nothing stimulated and pleased him more than the incontrovertible evidence of the exponential growth of population in the colonies that became the United States. What was there about the new world that would account for this startling difference? He knew—as did other luminaries of the time—that there were several obvious material differences (for example, climate, fertile land) but there was complete agreement that increase in population correlated with the happiness and welfare of the people. Jefferson returned again and again in his writings to this relationship. For Jefferson (and others), happiness could not be defined apart from the sense of independence, freedom, and self-worth. Jefferson wanted for others what he had gained for himself and what the new constitution sought to support and protect. Happiness was not a thing, not a now-and-then phenomenon, but a bedrock sense that one was free, self-respecting, and a foe of tyranny in all its many guises. No one had to tell Jefferson that life dealt one many unpleasant cards and, similarly, no one had to tell him that living under the yoke of tyranny of any kind was lethal to any enduring sense of happiness. If, as I think, he would be the last person to greet an increase in test scores as proof positive of progress, it would not be because he was allergic to counting, measuring, or numbers. As I indicated, he was enamored with numbers—what today we would call social statistics—because of their possible significance for explaining and judging the stated purposes of living.

It might seem from this opening that I am about to criticize the use of achievement tests, perhaps even suggest that we cease their use and substitute some other form of assessment. The fact is that I am not opposed to achievement tests; they can be informative and helpful. My argument rests on other grounds. Let me start with a question.

When your child graduates from high school, what is the one characteristic you would want your child to have? There are several major characteristics you would want your child to manifest but not all characteristics are equally influential over the course of a lifetime, influential in the sense of making life interesting and productive. That is not an easy question to answer precisely because as parents we know that several characteristics are important. But is there one characteristic that should take priority? I pose the question as I do because it requires you to come to grips with what you consider to be the overarching purpose of schooling. In his own way and times Jefferson answered the question unambiguously: the purpose of schooling was to enlarge and nurture a child's knowledge and understanding (they are not synonymous) of what it means to be responsibly free in a free society. Reading, writing, arithmetic, history, and so forth, were not ends in themselves but means to achieve an overarching purpose.

My answer to the question is in the spirit of all that Jefferson said, did, and wrote. When a child graduates from high school, I would want him or her to want to continue to learn more about self, others, and the world. Put in another way, *I would want all children to have at least the same level and quality of curiosity and motivation to learn and explore that they had when they began schooling*. It does not and should not make a difference whether the child is going to college or not; in either case the absence of wanting to learn and explore is symptomatic of the unexamined life; its presence is an asset the potentials of which are enormous, especially in a world that is complex, puzzling, and changing fast. The purpose of schooling is not to make students happy but to keep the fires of curiosity and exploration burning.

That, to some people, may sound idealistic, or fuzzy, or sentimental, or lacking direction for pedagogy, or all of these. To others what I have said will strike a responsive chord because they see themselves as locked into careers and existences that have effectively stifled or restricted or diluted their interest in and curiosity about their world; they get few or no kicks from what they think or do. That is the case with many people, however much or little their formal education. I must hasten to say that in no way am I suggesting that if schooling had kept the fires of curiosity and exploration burning, they would not as adults feel and think as they do. Such a claim could only reflect a pathological denial of the realities of contemporary living as well as of the imperfections of human beings. But I do claim two things. First, the curiosity, the motivation to learn and explore and feel awe, have for too many students (and I would say most) been brought to or near extinction by the time they graduate (and many, of course, do not manage to graduate) from high school. Many students are aware of this, which is why they regard schooling as a form of legally sanctioned child abuse, or like medicine you have to take even though you have no idea what your illness is. I am not indulging in hyperbole here, certainly not in regard to urban middle and high schools. Second, I do claim that if schooling took seriously the features of a context for productive learning, it would to an indeterminate extent and in an indeterminate number of people enrich their lives.

Initially, Jefferson would be no end gratified to learn about the dramatic increase in the number of young people whose education has extended to high school, college, and graduate school. He would be appalled to learn about the decrease in the number of people who vote in local, state, and national elections. One can imagine him saying, "How can one take satisfaction from the increase in years of schooling, when so many people are not interested in voting on the issues of the day, on matters crucial to the preservation of life, liberty, and the pursuit of happiness? Is it that they are truly uninterested? If so, how did this come about? Is it that when they finished schooling, they truly understood the history, struggles, and purposes of democratic living but thereafter their understanding and interest evaporated? Or were their years of schooling so superficial, so lacking in compellingness and personal significance, so irrelevant to their daily lives, as to unprepare them for their obligations as citizens who must be able to think critically, to give voice to their ideas, to stand up and to be counted for those ideas?"

How would we answer Jefferson? The answer, of course, would be very complex, and different people would give different emphases to this or that part of the answer. But no knowledgeable person would fail to criticize a schooling in which a large fraction of students view history as a museum of dead facts: it is not in the present, it has no significance for the future, it contributes nothing of use to the students' explanation of themselves, of others, of the world. Another way to put it is that the classroom and the school are organized on the basis of conceptions and values that do not permit the history of problems and struggles of democratic living to be experienced in those sites—that is, history took place at another time and place; it has no direct relevance in the here and now of people in schools. Some would go further, and say that it is far from the case that students derive facts—even dead facts—from the museum of history. They would point to surveys and reports—which appear in the mass media at least once a year—indicating that what students consider facts are frequently wrong—placing the Civil War in the eighteenth century, asserting that the United States went to war against the Soviet Union in World War II, and so forth. They would take some solace if it were the case that the dead facts in the museum were indeed facts. Jefferson would not have taken solace. His vision for education went far beyond the accumulation of facts. Facts take their meaning from what he called in the Declaration of Independence "these self-evident truths."

In the opening paragraphs of a recent paper, Darling-Hammond (1996) beautifully captures Jefferson's vision:

In the darkening days of the early McCarthy era, W.E.B. Du Bois [(1949) 1970] wrote these words:

Of all the civil rights for which the world has struggled
and fought for 5,000 years, the right to learn is undoubtedly
the most fundamental. . . . The freedom to learn . . . has
been bought by bitter sacrifice. And whatever we may think
of the curtailment of other civil rights, we should fight to the
last ditch to keep open the right to learn, the right to have
examined in our schools not only what we believe, but what
we do not believe; not only what our leaders say, but what
the leaders of other groups and nations, and the leaders of
other centuries have said. We must insist upon this to give
our children the fairness of a start which will equip them
with such an array of facts and such an attitude toward truth
that they can have a real chance to judge what the world is
and what its greater minds have thought it might be.

Du Bois knew, as did Thomas Jefferson when he conceived
our public education system, that America's capacity to survive
as a democracy relies not only on the provision of free public

education, although that is a crucial foundation; it rests on the kind of education that arms people with an intelligence capable of free and independent thought. In addition, it rests on an education that helps people to build common ground across diverse experiences and ideas. As Maxine Greene reminds us, if we are to create a public space for democracy, schools must consciously create community from the sharing of multiple perspectives and develop "the kinds of conditions in which people can be themselves." This is an education that seeks competence as well as community, that enables all people to find and act on who they are, what their passions, gifts, and talents may be, what they care about, and how they want to make a contribution to each other and the world.

These days, it is not fashionable to talk about education that is humane as well as rigorous, about the importance of caring for students and honoring each one's potential. These days the talk is tough: standards must be higher and more exacting, outcomes must be measurable and comparable, accountability must be hard-edged and punitive, and sanctions must be applied almost everywhere—to students and teachers, especially—although not to those whose decisions determine the possibilities for learning in schools. Yet, if we are to educate for democratic life, I believe we must be concerned about education that nurtures the spirit as well as the mind, so that each student finds and develops something of value on which to build a life while learning to value what others offer as well. It is the education each of us wants for our own children, but it is an education available to very few. Here, as always, John Dewey offers a central touchstone to guide our work: "What the best and wisest parent wants for his own child, that must the community want for all of its children. Any other ideal for our schools is narrow and unlovely; acted upon, it destroys our democracy."

So what does this quotation have to do with the supreme—and I use that word advisedly—importance placed on achievement test scores as *the* measure of the efficacy of schooling? Before you try to answer that question, you have to ask yourself how seriously you accept the words and vision of Jefferson, Dewey, Du Bois, and Darling-Hammond. And by seriously I mean how willing you are to judge what is by the substance of the vision. There has always been a tendency to use words like *vision* or *visionary* as containing goals and truths that are important but utopian, pie-in-the-sky, and not for this world as we think we know it. We are glad there are visionaries to remind us of the difference between what is and what ought to be, but we are so aware of the chasm that we resign ourselves to making do with what is, to accepting faltering measures that will seal over the extent of the chasm, or, worse yet, to allowing ourselves to believe that things are not as bad as they seem. The messages of visionaries are usually revolutionary in words and purpose. That certainly has been true for educational visionaries, but few people have the depth of feeling, drive, and courage to seek ways of acting in accord with those messages, and in the case of education there has been no visionary, political leadership to give voice and direction to new possibilities. Jefferson, of course, is the exception. He stimulated, informed, led, and acted. What should be vexing to the reader, as it should be to political leaders, is that what educational visionaries have said has been approximated in the heres and theres of this earth. That is what Darling-Hammond meant when she said "I believe we must be concerned about education that nurtures the spirit as well as the mind, so that each student finds and develops something of value on which to build a life while learning to value what others have to offer as well. It is an education each of us wants for our children, *but it is an education available to very few*" (italics mine). Very few is not enough—but it is sufficient to remind us of what can happen when visions are taken seriously.

Achievement tests are measures of facts—information contained in the curriculum and deemed important by the school. They also tell us about skill proficiency in regard to numbers, equations, formulas, and the like. If the scores on these tests meet an acceptable standard, it is assumed that the students have learned what they were supposed to learn and, no less important, that teachers have done their job well. But these scores do not tell us why the students got acceptable scores. What if we asked students to explain why they got acceptable scores? Students would find that a strange question. On numerous occasions I have asked students that question and the reaction has been puzzled silence. But when I persisted—it was not easy for them or me—the answers went this way: "We are sent to school to learn. The teacher knows what we have to learn and helps us learn it. Our job is to pay attention, do our homework, and show that we have done and learned what is expected of us. What teachers expect of us so do our parents. If you do not do what is expected of you, you are in trouble with your teachers and your parents. They will think you are dumb. So we work hard to show we are not dumb. We work hard and pass the tests."

Those answers were given by middle school children in suburbia. Some people will respond to those answers by saying plaintively, "If only *all* students came to school with those attitudes." And the parents of those students will be pleased that their children are going to a good school, and by *good* they mean that it is not a *bad* school where test scores are below acceptable standards. When surveys report that half or more parents are satisfied with the schools their children attend, and at the same time a larger percentage of them judge schools in general in unfavorable terms, one can legitimately assume that a major basis for their judgments is what they read in the mass media about the unacceptable tests scores of many students in many American schools. And, needless to say, they hear from the president on down that we must do what we can to elevate test scores. In the 1996 presidential campaign President Clinton, in speech after speech, emphasized that what he proposed would ensure that by the year 2000 every eight-year-old child will be able to read, by which he meant that test scores will confirm that his goal has been achieved.

Is it of no significance that not one of the middle school students I queried even faintly alluded to the possibility that their very acceptable test scores were in part because they found the subject matter intrinsically interesting, stimulating, and motivating enough to serve as goads to their thinking, working, learning? I cannot refute the criticism that I may have conducted the interviews in ways that did not make it easy for these students (on average twelve years of age) to express what I report as missing. I assume that the criticism is not about whether what I have reported is nonfactual— that is, I am not being accused of making up stories. The criticism is that the focus I adopted in the interviews may have obscured other aspects of the situation, aspects that would have shed a different light on what the students said, and whose absence may have led me to confuse facts with the truth. *That is precisely the limitation of test scores; they are facts that in and of themselves do not permit us to interpret those scores in a wider context. They do not have one and only one meaning and not all meanings are equally significant for interpretation and action.* To proceed as if the meaning of a test score is self-evident is to ignore the complexity of any form of human behavior. Test scores are facts that can be helpful if, and only if, we know something not only about the different psychological variables the test performance reflects but also about the social context of learning that makes those variables salient in the test situation—for example, attitudes toward self and learning, motivation to learn, peer relationships and ethos, the quest for identity and self-worth.

My parting question to the middle school students—which I asked in as offhand a manner as I was capable of—was, "Do you like, do you enjoy what you are learning in the different classes?" Most students looked at me again with puzzled silence. Several of the students asked, "Do you mean do we like school?" I would say no, that I was interested in whether they liked learning history, math, and so forth. With few exceptions, they expressed a degree of liking that varied from near zero to lukewarm. (There were, I must emphasize, exceptions. There are always exceptions, the equivalent of the "heres and theres" I referred to earlier). That, these students would say, did not mean they did not like some of their teachers or coming to school but that the subject matter they were learning held little interest for them. It was hard for me to avoid the conclusion that these bright students—whose test scores met or exceeded (most exceeded) acceptable standards—were not what you would call "turned on" learners or thinkers. To say that their test scores reflected the fruits of being in a context of productive learning is a form of mockery of language, concepts, and values.

What about students in the high schools of these suburban communities? I never talked with high school students as I did with those in middle schools. I observed a fair number of classes and I conversed with most of the teachers, the principal, and the assistant principals. The long and short of it is that these personnel were in near total agreement about number and types of students. First, approximately 5 percent of the students displayed a lack of respect for teachers and learning; they would rather be elsewhere than in school. They were far from stupid, they had good IQs, but they were either flunking their courses or getting a grade above flunk. Some were troublemakers, the rest were sullenly apathetic. Second, there were those students (approximately 20 percent) who came dutifully to school, caused no trouble, and did the bare minimum to earn low or mediocre grades. They, too, were not stupid, they were simply unmotivated, uninterested in achievement in school. Third, and by far the most numerous type, were those students who were motivated to get (and did get) better than mediocre grades but about many of whom it could not be said that they were thinkers. Their satisfaction came more from getting good grades than from any intrinsic satisfaction with the learning process. Good grades meant that they stood a chance of getting into the college of their choice. Fourth, approximately 3 percent to 5 percent of the students were those "who gladden the hearts of teachers." They had a degree of intellectual curiosity, a zest for learning, an independence of mind that, as one teacher said, "keeps a teacher going, and also keeps her on her toes."

In all respects my classroom observations in these suburban high schools confirmed what school personnel described. The problem for me is that their descriptions rather clearly implied that the reason too many students derived little or no intrinsic satisfaction from learning, and what made teaching them so difficult, was that these students lacked that mix of personal factors conducive to a zest for learning. Indeed, the implication was that given the social-economic-family backgrounds of the student body many more of them should be in the "gladden the hearts of teachers" category. I quite agree, but I also quite disagree. Sitting in those classrooms was as boring to me as it was for most of the students. I am not being critical of teachers. Teachers teach the way they have been taught to teach, but what they have been taught produces the polar opposite of a context for productive learning. I am in no way asserting that contexts of learning and living outside school are not of momentous importance. Nor am I suggesting that if by some miracle schools approximated better the creation and sustaining of contexts of productive learning, all (or even most) students would be in the "gladden the heart" category. There are limits to what one can expect from schooling if contexts outside school are not facilitating or supporting, contexts over which schools have little or no control. But I have no doubt that a significant number of students would find schooling more enlivening and enriching.

I have deliberately started with my observations and comments of suburban schools because of the widespread opinion that the test scores of their students are a measure of student interest in and zest for thinking and learning. It is an opinion, but it is also a myth. The significance of those test scores is not as self-evident as people would like to believe. This is not to say that those test scores are without meaning but rather to say that *any* test score has more than one meaning and if we do not pursue those meanings— if we unreflectively assume that the score has but one obvious meaning—we end up making a serious error. To say that test scores tell us all we need to know about the quality of student thought, of the significance and use a student makes of the subject matter the test assesses, is simple—and, as Mencken warns us, wrong. Everyone, including presidents, other political leaders, and educators knows this. That may sound strange, so let me explain.

Back in the late 1950s, Americans were dumbfounded when the Soviet Union orbited a space capsule before we did. It was a major blow to national pride and it aroused anxiety about what it portended, militarily and otherwise. What had been muted criticism about our schools became loud and clamorous. The indictment led to diverse actions in Washington. Two of those actions are most relevant here. One of them was an explicit recognition that achievement tests (or intelligence tests) tell nothing about the creativity of students. It had long been known that the correlation between conventional test scores and demonstrated creativity in work performance among different groups of professionals (for example, architects) was by no means very high. In any event, the orbiting of the first Russian sputnik led to a lot of research, mostly federally funded, to develop measures of creativity. It is not necessary for me to describe and assess that research to make the point that conventional test scores have long been known to be uninformative about cognitive and personality variables (interests, motivations, hobbies, idiosyncrasies) that either enter into test performance or enlarge our understanding of a student's test score. The fact is that the theorizing and research on these variables have had no influence whatsoever on the overarching importance schools place on achievement test scores. For a period of fifteen years I conducted a research program on the role of test anxiety in the test performance of school students (Sarason, Hill, and Zimbardo, 1964; Sarason and Hill, 1966). The evidence was incontrovertible: the level of test anxiety was a factor in test performance. Varying the test situation so as to increase or decrease levels of anxiety was a difference that made a difference in test scores. That was the case with groups of students who had very high IQs and even more the case with groups with average or below-average IQs. We conducted that research in four different school systems. We made our findings known to school personnel. It aroused no interest, it changed no practice, their sole interest was achievement test scores.

The second consequence of the Russian sputnik was that it galvanized federal and state political leaders to increase funding for the identification of and special programs or classes for so-called gifted students, which in practice always referred to students with very high IQs (usually but not always very highly correlated with high achievement test scores). For a reason I shall discuss later these classes were of special interest to me. I visited, observed some of these classrooms, and interviewed the teachers. The focus of my interest was the range of individual differences teachers reported observing in how students perform in these classes, given that they vary relatively little in IQ. I paraphrase their answers. "They vary all over the lot and in ways that surprised me. Let me first say that they are relatively easy to be with and to teach. With some of them I knew by the end of the first week what their interests were, the books they were reading or had read, what subjects or topics they wanted to pursue. Some had interests that scared me because I did not know if I could be of real help to them. How could I be of help to somebody who had special interests and knowledge that I did not have? I call them the self-starters. With others I still don't know what goes on in their heads, what interests them, whether they have a sense of direction. I sometimes wonder whether they have a low level of motivation, or that they lack self-confidence, or that they expect to be given a direction. They learn quickly, they do what you tell them to do, they almost always do it well, but they don't seem to show any visible satisfaction from what they do. They are definitely not self-starters and they are not creative. If they are outstanding on IQ and achievement tests, they are not high on anything else I can observe; they may have a gift but they display little of it. And, finally, there are two or three in this class [usually twelve to fifteen students] who are average or below, regardless of what their test scores are. Their work is sloppy or wrong or illogical, or just plain mediocre."

My special interest in gifted programs derived from my experience in my first professional job in an institution for mentally retarded individuals. In my several years there I probably tested several hundred residents of all ages, appearance, and background. Because the job was in Connecticut's rural nowhere, World War II was on and transportation virtually nonexistent, and I was required to live on site, I got to know most of the residents very well. By the time I left that position I had come to two conclusions. The first was that it was both foolhardy and irresponsible to use test scores from standardized tests as the major, or primary, let alone sole, basis for planning programs for individuals. In numerous publications I have presented many cases where that point is illustrated. (That point had long been made by other psychologists, and as recently as 1996, Sternberg made the same point very compellingly on the basis of a multifaceted research program.) So, for example, in those years (1942–1945) the state could deny admission to an individual with an IQ of 71 and raise no question at all about admitting someone with an IQ of 69. An IQ of 70 was the cut-off point; all else was commentary.

If the first conclusion is in the category of glimpses of the obvious (to working psychologists at least), the second conclusion is not: *There is virtually no systematic evidence that the quality and level of problem solving in test situations is at all highly correlated with level and quality of problem solving in naturally occurring (that is, noncontrived) situations.* Obviously, if that correlation is not high, you should be gun-shy about unreflectively overinterpreting test scores.

The day after I started to work in the institution, one of the residents ran away. A posse was formed to look for the person. Aside from alerting the state police as well as the few people who lived in a nearby tiny village, we combed the woods surrounding the institution. That was standard procedure. In my first year there were upward of twenty-five runaways, some of whom we never located. Many were not caught until they arrived at their homes miles away. It dawned on me one day that I had tested most of those runaways and that one of the tests was the Porteus

Mazes, which are graded in difficulty and require the person to draw a continuous line from a central starting point to the exit without going into a cul-de-sac. The Porteus Mazes were a test of foresight and planning. In all but a few cases the runaways had been given the test. To my surprise a majority of them had failed all but the easiest mazes and in some instances had failed even those.

How had these individuals planned and executed a successful runaway from a closely supervised setting? To accomplish that required foresight and planning hardly or not at all in evidence on the mazes on the test.

When in the 1960s I began to work in ghetto schools, I saw more examples of the lack of correlation between learning in school and learning outside school, between unmotivated learning in classrooms and motivated learning outside school.

As I said earlier, I am not one who believes that test scores are meaningless. My quarrel is with the assumption that an achievement test score permits us to make generalizations independent of attitude, motivation, interest, and context. The test scores of students in a suburban school may be the highest in the state and that surely should be a source of satisfaction. But does one stop there? Is it nit-picking or irrelevant to ask what those scores tell us about how students digest, regard, and utilize the knowledge and skills those tests sample? Is one an unseemly critic in saying that the satisfaction school personnel and parents take from those elevated test scores would discernibly decrease if they learned that many students experienced school learning as uninteresting, boring, pointless, irrelevant to their understanding of what life is about?

William James once said, "Ideas (which themselves are but parts of our experience) become true just insofar as they help us get into satisfactory relation with other parts of our experience." John Dewey (another pragmatist) said, "Since democracy stands in principle for free interchange, for continuity, it must develop a theory of knowledge which sees in knowledge the method by which one experience is made available in giving direction and meaning to another." Those two highly similar statements articulate a criterion by which to judge the efficacy of schooling in that the emphasis is not on discrete facts and knowledge as measured by conventional tests but on the process whereby different aspects of knowledge and experience interpenetrate, take on new meanings, open up new vistas, and give one a sense of growth. We do not have tests for that process, not because such tests are in principle impossible to devise but because of our tradition-bound inability to distinguish between knowledge and knowing. What our achievement tests measure is *knowledge,* which is external to the learner. It tells us nothing about *knowing,* which is the active, motivated process by which we own, possess, and utilize knowledge so that it does not remain external but is internally assimilated. What I have earlier called contexts for productive learning are contexts in which the difference between knowledge and knowing is always center stage. Because knowledge can be and so frequently is regurgitated—a kind of memory game—is no warrant for believing that what has been regurgitated signifies what we hope it means: productive assimilation and utilization. The evidence is otherwise and that says as much about contexts of unproductive learning as it does about learners, and I contend that it says more about the former than about the latter.

Achievement test scores are used as if they are barometers of the educational health of individuals, schools, and the nation. I use the word *health* to make a point as obvious as it is important, because in matters of health, judgments are never made on the basis of a single test. A normal body temperature never permits the conclusion that a person is well. That conclusion is permissible only if other signs of illness are negative. What we call an annual physical examination requires a variety of tests, and even so it is not infrequent that pathological symptoms appear soon after the examination. Indeed, the more that is learned about the human body, the more tests are devised to spot signs of potential malfunction. In fact, the medical community has been criticized for conducting too many tests and thus increasing medical costs. However, that criticism, which may contain a kernel of truth, ignores the fact that if physicians have learned anything, it is that the appearance of health is not synonymous with the reality of health; things may be going on that the tests of appearances do not reveal. As I have indicated, that is why elevated achievement test scores may or may not be a sign of educational health. Similarly, and not facetiously, it does not follow that because a person has accumulated a fortune, he or she uses that wealth productively, has a sense of personal growth and self-respect, enjoys the present and looks forward to the future. There are magazines that annually tell us who are the fifty or one hundred wealthiest people in the country, and we unreflectively respond to such wealth as we do to schools where test scores are elevated: "They have it made." When we say that, we are unaware that we are attributing significances to those single numbers that may or may not be justified. Need I elaborate on the statement that in the case of those numbers the evidence supporting justification is, to say the least, shaky in the extreme? Wish fulfillment is no substitute for caution or skepticism.

Why is it that in regard to the educational health of the nation we obsessively and compulsively rivet on single test scores while in regard to the health of the national economy we employ or actively seek and devise scores of indices? The president and the top economic advisers would *never* pass judgment on economic health on the basis of one, two, or three measures of economic activity. Let me list only some of the most frequently used indices:

- Gross National Product
- Change in level of employment and unemployment
- Inventory levels
- Consumer confidence
- Orders for durable goods
- Work productivity
- Housing starts
- Sales of new and old homes
- Changes in interest rates
- Report of the National Association of Purchasing Managers
- Rates of inflation

Why is it that beginning early in this century there was a steady increase in government interest in how to fathom the health and direction of the national economy? Why after World War II was the presidential Council of Economic Advisors created? The answer has its positive and negative aspects. The negative aspect derived from the recognition that heretofore utilized tests of economic activity had been, singly or in combination, grossly inadequate, or misleading, or poorly weighted, the result being that political leaders were unprepared for events with serious adverse consequences for the nation—for example, the Great Depression. Not only were they unprepared but they had no secure basis for actions to deal with those consequences. In brief, available tests of economic performance were part of the problem and not part of the solution. The positive aspect was the recognition that there was a vast difference between numbers and their social-psychological meanings. That is to say, an index of economic performance (for example, changes in rate of inflation) took on significance because of what it suggested about what people were thinking and doing. Our economic system is not a mechanical, inanimate one and any test of any aspect of the system is presumed to say something important about people's thinking and behavior, something having import about the direction the economy may take. Since that something is by no means self-evident, it requires that one seek to devise more tests of its nature. Thousands of economists spend thousands of hours in the effort to devise more sensitive ways of extracting meaning from numbers and relating the meaning of one set of numbers to the meaning of others. Even so, as Cassidy (1996) recently pointed out, most of the tests of economic health or activity have a poor track record. One reason, he points out, is that economists have become so enamored with utilizing advanced mathematics in developing economic tests that what they devise is light years away from what real people and groups actually think and do. Indeed, one reason economics is called the "dismal science" is that it rests on a psychology that is as nonsensical as it is invalid.[1]

---

1.   In November 1996, as this chapter was being written, a controversy had arisen among economists and political leaders about the calculation, meanings, and use of the Rate of Inflation, the Commodity Price Index, the Gross National Product, and Productivity. In principle and social import the issues are identical to those I have discussed in regard to achievement tests. It is not a controversy about numbers but about what those numbers overlook and, therefore, how they mislead. No one asserts that these tests of economic health are unnecessary. Many do assert that these indices are insensitive to changes in how people think and act in response to changes in technology, social attitudes, and demography. So, for example, if Gross National Product increases in part because of huge outlays in coping with AIDS or drugs, does it make sense to conclude that economic health has increased?

My point is that we use achievement test scores as if they tell us how school-acquired knowledge is remembered, regarded, and utilized by students, as if it is not necessary to know other than the test scores, as if we have learned nothing whatever about productive learning, its contexts, its role in everyday living, planning, adapting. The irony here is that many teachers agree with my argument. Whether you are a public school or university teacher—and I taught in the university for forty-five years—you have to be unusually dense to believe that test scores are revealing of how a student assimilates, interrelates, and uses the domain of knowledge the test is supposed to sample. It used to be that teaching for the test was frowned upon because it subverted the purpose of schooling to help students think—that is, not to be a narrow memory game that ran roughshod over the interests, attitudes, and motivation of students. Today there are teachers, school administrators, and public officials who see nothing wrong in teaching for the test. For them the difference between knowledge and knowing is a difference that makes no difference—and furthermore it is a difference beloved of academics, philosophers, and theoreticians, whom they regard as members of an impractical breed. I cannot refrain from saying to these critics and name callers that my impracticality has not prevented me over the decades from making predictions about the fate of the reform movement that have been far more accurate than those of these critics who in response to failure continue to come up with bromides they pray will elevate achievement test scores. The latest example is their advocacy of clear standards, preferably national ones, which students will have to meet, and meet means better achievement test scores. Why contexts of *unproductive* learning will enable students to meet these new standards is a question that escapes them as it does me.

In an earlier chapter I said there were several questions the president could and should ask a commission to study and answer. On the basis of what I have said in this chapter I would add the following questions: What is the evidence for the policy and practice of assessing educational outcomes by the scores on conventional achievement tests? How well do these tests indicate the quality of what has been learned—that is, what do they reveal about how that learning has been assimilated, digested, utilized, and how it has motivated students? Are we justified in continuing to employ these tests as we have before gaining clarity and agreement about the overarching purpose of schooling?

The questions are of two kinds. The first is empirical in the sense that they call for an assessment of evidence for present practices. The second is a combination of the moral, political, and philosophical in that we are required to confront the all-important question: What kinds of *people* do we want our schools to shape?

I must remind the reader that these and the earlier questions are significant only if you believe that schools as we know them are in need of radical transformation and that their past intractability to change speaks volumes both about their rigidities and our tinkering. And if you believe that, it is because in the quiet of our nights we feel that the society we should be will never take shape unless schools (among other things—for example, hopelessness about employment) become other than what they are. Unless those changes begin to occur I predict that our social ills will worsen. If you listen to speeches of presidents and others in high office, they are making the same predictions. Absent presidential-political leadership, their predictions and mine unfortunately stand an excellent chance of being confirmed.

Chapter Five

The Context of Productive Learning

In the past few years, forty-eight states and the District of Columbia have committed themselves to setting statewide standards for students to meet for promotion and graduation. In some states the enabling legislation was an initiative of governors, some of whom gained national recognition for educational leadership. On the national level, President Clinton has spoken favorably about national standards. What accounts for the speed and force of these developments? Why now and not five, ten, or more years ago? The answer is predictably complex, so much so that it is reason enough to expect that actions that ignore this complexity will be a source of disappointment.

Let me begin with a glimpse of the obvious. No one will dispute that in the past three decades we have witnessed pervasive social, racial, gender, sexual, and technological changes (Sarason, 1995a). That is another way of saying that earlier standards for judging the behavior of individuals and groups changed. No major institution in our society escaped changing in some ways. Some people viewed these changes favorably; many did not—and their conflicts continue today. No societal institution was pressured to change more than the schools, especially in our cities, where heated conflicts concerned who should teach, what should be taught, who should exercise decision-making powers. Schools and their personnel were seen as rigid, insensitive to both students and communities, unimaginative, and self-serving. Even before the social changes became manifest, curriculum reformers (mostly from universities) explicitly criticized the ability, preparation, and practices of educators. The consequence of all of this was that over the past several decades scores of billions of dollars were spent on thousands of programs to develop new curricula, upgrade the quality and preparation of educators, support relevant research, and institute compensatory and preventive programs for disadvantaged children. Although it is fair to say that these expenditures reflected an optimism that schools could be improved, it is also fair to say that throughout these decades attitudes toward educators were at best ambivalent and at worst very derogatory. School personnel had never been accorded the respect given to those in other professions, and as the reform years went on and desired goals were nowhere in sight, the assignment of blame was directed to teachers and administrators. "If a student is not learning, the teacher is not teaching." "Accountability begins with the teacher." These and other, similar statements were heard and approved by many people who were puzzled and depressed by the general failure of the reform movement.

The fact is that schools had, like every other societal institution, changed (in similar ways) and they became more accepting of behavior and quality of performance they ordinarily would not have accepted. More correctly, they sought to adapt—they felt required to adapt—to the changed attitudes of students, parents, and administrators, and to a plethora of ideas and programs of advocates of educational reform. It was not permissiveness if by that you meant that educators took the stance "To hell with standards, there is nothing we can do to maintain standards." On the contrary, their stance was "The social world has changed. Schools have changed. We should try new practices that will help us help more kids realize their potential." It was not the intent of the reformers to lower standards but rather to make learning more interesting and salient to students, to increase their motivation to learn. So, for example, those who developed new math curricula in no way sought to lower standards. They knew well that too many students were math illiterates or had been turned off from anything mathematical. Their new math curricula were designed to make math interesting and a spur to flexible thinking. The content of these curricula was very different from the traditional texts but it was assumed that it would increase rather than decrease mathematical interest and proficiency.

It did not work out the way the reformers and general public had hoped. Achievement test scores seemed slowly but steadily to decline, then plateau, or go up a couple of points in one subject area while other subject areas remained depressingly the same. No one who reads in the mass media about the reports of local, state, and federal surveys of educational performance has cause to be optimistic, even though the sponsors of these reports strive valiantly to pinpoint certain findings that potentially may provide a basis for optimism.

Why the current emphasis on clear and stringent standards? The most general answer is that it is a kind of backlash against post–World War II social change, the hallmark of which has been a perceived alteration in standards in *all* arenas of society, by no means only in education. Divorce rates, juvenile and adult crime rates, pervasive use of drugs, child physical and sexual abuse, pornography, teenage pregnancy, sexually explicit popular music, violence in movies and on TV, popular TV talk shows in which almost all individuals relate their (heretofore) most personal titillating proclivities and actions—each of these and more represent changes in standards of thinking and action. I know of no political leader who views those changes in standards with approval. Some of them say, "As a nation we have lost our way," or "We are no longer a nation with a shared set of values (standards)," or "This is not a country that can allow individuals and groups to do whatever they decide to. There are limits, boundaries, and standards, and if we do not observe them, they will destroy us." So when achievement test scores began their decline and violence in schools increased and the salaries of teachers discernibly increased and no reform effort had a generalizing effect, and when achievement test scores in our cities remained abysmally low and the dropout rate in city schools remained pitifully high and it became obvious that the social-vocational implications of the widening gulf between city and suburbs was truly frightening, it should occasion no surprise that political leaders and others—including, as we shall soon see, some educators—concluded that educational standards had been allowed to deteriorate (or "dumbed down," as Senator Moynihan would say) and that new, clear, stringent standards had to be proclaimed and adhered to.[1] And, it was asserted, these new standards would give needed direction to teachers at the same time it would confront students with the realities of "shaping up or shipping out."

In his *New York Times* piece of September 29, 1996, Albert Shanker's column is titled "The Real Solution." Here are some excerpts:[2]

> Yet while most states are working to develop higher academic standards, only 15 have standards in the core subjects—English, math, history, and science—that could form the basis for a rigorous curriculum. The reason is that many of the standards are vague and general and lacking in content. Take this middle-school math standard from Nebraska: "Students should be able to discover and develop formulas." Which formulas? The standard does not say. A social studies standard from Massachusetts suffers from a similar fuzziness: "Students will explain how a variety of factors can lead to the outcome of an event."
>
> Unless they make clear *which* mathematical formulas students should master and *which* events in history students should learn

---

1.   Few things reflected the more general social change and spurred a revival of the standards controversy more vividly than acts of violence in and around school buildings. Today in Connecticut it is by no means unusual for security guards and police to be in schools. And, it should be emphasized, that is the case in the schools of some of Connecticut's most affluent enclaves (Cavanaugh, 1997).

2.   Shanker is an educational leader, but he is also a political one, situated as he is in Washington and having easy access to an elected officialdom that has easy access to him. Mr. Shanker gets around; that is his job. By virtue of his column, which is paid for by the American Federation of Teachers, he is the only educational-political, non–publicly elected person who has a national audience. Newspapers pay for columnists who write daily or weekly about politics, economics, cooking, religion, literature, the arts, legal issues, wine, and so forth, but not about education. Why that is so is less important here than that it is so and speaks to why the general public has such a superficial understanding of educational issues.
   Albert Shanker died in February 1997. See my notes about him in the preface of this book.

about, standards will be useless. They won't offer teachers guidance about the material they need to cover or tell parents what they should expect their children to learn. Indeed, standards like these will offer little improvement over the system we now have. This will be a tragedy for all our students but particularly for those inner-city schools because they are the ones who stand to benefit most from a challenging curriculum. . . .

The states are off to a promising start. The majority have developed good standards in at least one subject, and some have exemplary standards that others can look to as models. But states need to do more than raise standards; they must also be encouraged to attach stakes to these standards. Students need to know that the hard work they put in will count—both in school, for promotion and graduation, and when they look for a job or apply for entrance to a college. Otherwise, the highest standards and the richest curriculum are unlikely to solve our problems.

Several things are noteworthy and praiseworthy in those excerpts. For one thing, Shanker exposes the difference between vacuous abstractions, generalizations that are essentially inkblots, and concrete standards. (The Ten Commandments are concrete standards and their relation to action quite explicit; whether you agree with them is one thing, what they call for is quite another.) For another thing, he alerts the reader to the fact that changing curricula is easy—that is, you substitute one book or manual for another, but what is important is what and how the new curriculum communicates to and is experienced by teachers and students. Finally, Shanker, as he always does, asserts that given the deplorable performance of our city schools, what happens there is crucially important.

There are, however, some very troubling features in that column. The first is the title—"The Real Solution." Elsewhere in the column he writes, "Most states believe that school reform must begin with higher academic standards." In other words, higher standards are a *beginning* of a solution, not the solution itself. What follows or accompanies the beginning is no less fateful than your starting point. We have learned a good deal from the debacle of the new curricula introduced in the 1960s. But there is another troubling feature, ultimately the most misleading, and that is that in the social arena we are never dealing with solutions in the sense that four divided by two has a solution. We are always dealing with problems that require us to accept approximations, make corrections dictated by experience, pay respect to our imperfections and a social world we do not and cannot control, and maybe even to begin all over again. To call higher standards a solution guarantees disappointment, name-calling, and unproductive controversy. In the post–World War II era we have had a surfeit of such so-called solutions, which is why many people have concluded that improving schools is a waste of time, money, and interest. A friend of mine put it this way: "In the 1996 presidential election, the voter turnout was scandalously low. People felt it made no difference because they saw the mess and gridlock in Washington as having a life of its own, impervious to what the electorate felt. People have come to view schools the way they do the Beltway: Unchangeable."

As one would expect, Shanker says nary a word about the adequacy and variations among teachers in terms of their knowledge, pedagogy, preparation, and understanding of contexts of productive learning. Indeed, in none of his columns does he address these considerations. One is left with the impression that these considerations played no role in the past failures of the reform movement—that is, teachers in general had been okay but it was the reformers and policymakers, ever responsive to the winds of educational fashion and the pressures of political correctness, who misled teachers. There is a kernel of truth to that but that in no way means that other considerations were insignificant in their effects. And that point leads into a final troublesome feature requiring me to say that Shanker makes an error he criticizes in regard to the fuzzy language of standards.

Shanker says that clear, higher standards are necessary "particularly for those in inner-city schools because they are the ones who stand to benefit most from a *challenging* curriculum" (italics mine). If no one is opposed to clear, concrete standards, neither is anyone opposed to a challenging curriculum. That, of course, begs the question. We ought to be asking how we should define *challenging*. Like many other pundits, Shanker avoids considering that point. Obviously, and I do mean obviously, when we use the word *challenging*, we are referring to a particular kind of human relationship in which one individual (or group) calls into question an assertion, behavior, or rights of another individual (or group). The challenge contains a message, written (for example, in the form of a curriculum) or unwritten, but in either case it is assumed or expected that the individual being challenged will not respond neutrally—that is, not disinterestedly, cavalierly, or unemotionally. Indeed, if you consult your dictionary, you are very likely to find the word *dispute* in the definition. However you use the word *challenging,* you clearly imply that those being challenged experience diverse reactions. The written curriculum is or can be at best minimally challenging. Whether it is more than that depends on the pedagogy of the teacher, and that pedagogy reveals how the teacher conceives of the differences between productive and unproductive contexts of learning. There are inspiring and uninspiring teachers, challenging and unchallenging ones, psychologically sensitive and insensitive ones, creative and unimaginative ones. The point, of course, is that you can have a written curriculum geared to clear, concrete, rigorous standards that is taught in a way that is the opposite of challenging.

One of the ways of characterizing the post–World War II reform movement is that it sought to make classroom learning interesting and challenging for students. For example, the proponents of the new math said that math classes were among the most unjoyous places on earth and the revised curricula would alter that. Learning math should and could be a joy. It is remarkable that there was only one study of that claim. It was done by my late wife, Dr. Esther Sarason, who had to conclude that joy was the last word that came to mind in observing these classes. Similarly, Susskind (1969) found that the average number of student questions was two in a forty-minute period—it could have been one student asking two questions—and the average of teacher questions ranged from 40 to 150, a finding that violates *any* conception of productive learning that has ever appeared in print.

The point here is that challenge is in the eye of the beholder, and one of those beholders is the challenged, the student. How that is to be determined is beyond my present purposes. The important point is that it is never (or very rarely) determined by teachers. Few things in education have gone unresearched—but one of them is the formal and informal ways of determining why, how, and to what degree students experience a classroom as challenging. My own, very provisional definition of *challenge* is that it arouses curiosity, questions are provoked, those questions are articulated, there is give-and-take, and the students see themselves and the problem in a new way that arouses new questions and interest in the spirit of the more you know, the more you need to know. That is what I would call the psychological-pedagogical curriculum. Productive learning literally produces new knowledge and attitudes about self and subject matter, it alters in some way the relation between what is inside and outside, the subjective and the objective.

I am sure Albert Shanker would agree with me, because after he had seen the movie *Mr. Holland's Opus* he wrote a column about it that explicitly and implicitly agrees with what I have said. He does not say anything about how many Mr. Hollands there are in classrooms or why Mr. Holland had to be hit over the head by repeated failure to challenge his students before he inchoately understood the difference between productive and unproductive learning. Nor does Shanker indict the preparatory programs that produce the Mr. Hollands of the educational world. After all, as president of one of the two major teachers unions in the country, he is understandably constrained from criticizing teachers.[3]

On the entire cover page of the *New York Times Magazine* for October 27, 1996, are examples of items from a multiple-choice achievement test. At the bottom of the page in a contrasting orange is "What Really Matters in Education" by Sara Mosle, a former New York City elementary school teacher and now a contributing writer for the magazine. On the first page of the article is the heading: "The answer is national standards." The word *standards* is in bold orange. "Education is a campaign issue without a focus. The school reform that really matters is not vouchers or charter schools or breaking the unions or wiring the classrooms. It is a curriculum set in Washington, and monitored in every town and city through testing."

The beginning paragraphs of her article are devoted to her experience of conducting a mandated, hands-on science unit about boats and "why things float." By the end of the day the children, the

---

3.   As I have clearly stated in all my previous writings, to take potshots at teachers would be an egregious example of blaming the victim. They teach the way they have been taught and it is a way that the culture, organization, and size of schools uniformly support and reinforce.

teacher, and the classroom were untidy messes. Another teacher poked her head in the room and, incredulous, asked, "You're actually *doing* this with so many kids?" Mosle writes, "[I] nodded weakly, my clothes covered in clay, my hair frazzled, the classroom a mess." She later learned that other teachers simply did demonstration experiments in front of their classes. She wryly adds, "So much for hands on learning."

In telling us of that experience, Mosle provides us with the following information:

- This elementary school contained sixteen hundred children in a building designed for half that number.
- The reading and math scores were so low that there was the real possibility that the school would be taken over by the state.
- She had thirty-two students in a classroom too small to employ a cooperative learning pedagogy that she had seen demonstrated in her preparatory program.
- The students were children of immigrant parents, many of whom could not speak English. Apparently, a fair number of students did not speak or comprehend English well.
- There were no background materials for teachers, no histories of science, "no interesting tales about real scientists to inspire kids."
- "We were supposed to be inculcating a love of reading in our kids but they almost never got a chance to read nonfiction. Yes, yes, I could haul in books from the local library, create research projects from scratch, design a thematic unit around the 'Titanic' [the why do boats float theme], but curriculum building of this sort takes exceptional amounts of time, energy and devotion."

Mosle has told us more than she realizes. In the very brief comments I shall make, the reader should not lose sight of the fact that what Mosle describes is by no means unusual in our urban schools, although, as usual, everything (good or bad) is magnified in New York City.

- *How should one view political leadership—local, state, national— that countenances the situation she describes?* It is not that they do not know the situation. It has been described to them countless times.

• *Why should national standards change anything in Mosle's school?* Do we really need more tests (or more monitoring from the state or federal government) to tell us what we already know: that existing, let alone elevated, standards are not being met? Does that tell us what needs to or should be done?

• *Can we trust a puzzled, insensitive political leadership whose past efforts at reform have failed to come up with a new understanding of schools and reform failures?*

• *Why did Mosle's preparatory program have her observe cooperative learning without requiring her to meet a minimal level of competence (standard) in that pedagogy?* She reports that she saw demonstrations of cooperative learning "but always in small 'alternative' settings, with lots of supplies and assistance and managed by teachers who had developed and managed their methods over years." And, I should add, it appears that her preparatory program was little if at all helpful about teaching in the kind of school she found herself. I assume that the preparatory program had standards she easily met. But those standards were not relevant to what she faced in a real classroom with real problems.

• *What should we make of her comment that it was only later—after the science unit debacle—that she learned that other teachers ignored a hands-on approach and stood in front of the students and did the unit?* That suggests an absence of collegiality that sustains a sink-or-swim ambience and sets the stage for teacher burnout, which is high in our city schools. I could not read her account without the imagery of the movie *Mr. Holland's Opus* coming to mind.

Given the priority Mosle gives to national standards monitored from Washington, I have to regard her article as a kind of non sequitur because she gives us no basis for the expectation that national standards will have any impact on the conditions she describes or deal with the comments to her article I just made.

Let us look at standards by examining two well-known approaches to reform, which differ (among other things) in regard to the *content* of standards. I refer to the work and writings of Sizer (1996) and Hirsch (1987).

Sizer has long been a vociferous critic of a drill-memorize pedagogy that ignores the curiosity and interests of students and produces boring, uninteresting classrooms as well as students who are given no basis for how to think, how ideas take on meaning only in relation to other ideas. That pedagogy, Sizer asserts, guarantees that students will not learn how to think. The only clear meaning of a high school diploma is that it is evidence that a student has sat in classrooms for twelve years and has met required standards of behavior and subject matter. That means, of course, that Sizer looks at conventional achievement tests as signifying little about how students think, how they regard both content and learning. Sizer is no mindless critic of content. Indeed, one of his principles is that "less is more," meaning that (in high school) there should be fewer subject matter courses so that there is more time for teaching subject matter in an interdisciplinary way, interrelating ideas that are connected in history and contemporary life. That requires that the one teacher–one class tradition be altered so that teachers will work in teams. They must have more of a role in determining what and how subject matter is taught. What standards should be employed for judging student achievement? Sizer recommends portfolios, exhibits, and special projects that the faculty judges in terms of quality of substance, industry, organization, originality, and independence of thinking.

Hirsch is appalled by what students do not know: content or facts that any thinking, mature, responsible citizen must or should know. In the spirit of Jefferson, Hirsch rightly believes that a citizenry ignorant of basic facts of national and world history, as well as of the contemporary world, is a citizenry incapable of sustaining what is best in our society. Others have pointed this out—but Hirsch achieved celebrity because of the way and force with which he alerted the public to the scandalous ignorance of students generally, not only in our city schools. How does one account for such ignorance? Obviously, Hirsch concludes, what passes for teaching and learning in our schools is irresponsibly misguided in the extreme. And, like Sizer, Hirsch developed a program (for elementary schools) to demonstrate a pedagogy and achievement test standards, as clear as those Shanker advocated, by which to judge performance. Hirsch is caustically critical of the Sizer approach, which advocates interdisciplinary instruction, hands-on units, cooperative learning, portfolios, and the like, as much because they are employed badly as because they give second place to the acquiring of basic cultural knowledge. Hirsch gives first place to recitation, memorization, standardized tests, and other traditional devices. Verbal instruction should be an essential and even dominant focus of schooling. Hirsch sees people like Sizer as obfuscating "progressives" who despite their good intentions contribute to the further dilution of the significance and quality of standards. Sizer sees people like Hirsch as "traditionalists" incapable of understanding how their orientation has produced the mess Sizer has observed and described.

It would seem that the Sizer versus Hirsch controversy is kin to the Hatfields versus the McCoys, believers versus atheists, psychoanalysts versus behaviorists. Nevertheless, in what follows I feel secure in assuming that both Sizer and Hirsch favor classrooms that are challenging and interesting to students. Put negatively, neither would look favorably on classrooms where students were semisomnolent, or passive, or unduly conformist, or ritualistically going through the motions. After all, Hirsch is a professor at Jefferson's University of Virginia. Sizer (a Yalie) was headmaster of Andover Academy, dean of Harvard's Graduate School of Education, and recently retired as professor of education at Brown University.

You would expect that a Sizer classroom would look very different from a Hirsch one. Let me turn, then, to a report in *U.S. News & World Report* (Toch and Daniel, 1996, pp. 58–64), a report that is surprisingly instructive and balanced in that it very accurately presents the obvious written differences between Hirsch and Sizer, and at the same time describes classroom similarities. Here are excerpts about a Sizer school:

> The atmosphere at Hope Essential High School in Providence, R.I., where Sizer's ideas flourish, reflects his emphasis on developing students' minds. Housed on the top floor of an inner-city building, the 370 mostly African-American and Latino students of this school-within-a-school move through their day in 90–minute sessions. There are few textbooks. Teachers rarely lecture. The curriculum is divided into four large blocks—math, science, English and social studies. In many courses, students study only a few topics intensively. . . .
>
> At Hope Essential, breaking the school day into large blocks makes relationships between students and teachers more personal.

In turn, student attendance is up, discipline problems are down. Interdisciplinary instruction gives students a richer understanding of what they are learning, exemplified in student exhibitions so important to Sizer as alternatives to standardized tests. Last year, with the O.J. Simpson trial in the news, a month's study of Shakespeare's *Othello* in an 11th-grade English class at Hope Essential culminated not in a multiple-choice test but in a mock trial of the Moor for Desdemona's murder. Students explored the tragedy's insights into marriage, jealousy and responsibility. Their tasks included reciting portions of the play, writing papers in the form of opening and closing legal arguments and a host of other activities.

Such intensive study pays off: Nearly 90 percent of Hope Essential's students are admitted to college, up from 18 percent at Hope High School before Sizer arrived.

At schools Hirsch has nurtured, like Roland Park Elementary and Middle School on Baltimore's West Side, his philosophy is on display. Students in Regina White's fifth-grade classroom perform a scene, theater-in-the-round style, from *Don Quixote*. Elizabeth Aliberti's sixth-grade pupils practice songs from the musical version of *Oliver Twist*. Each day is an expedition into core knowledge, from Bach to Michelangelo to the science of rainbows.

Roland Park's curriculum is a far cry from the school's pre-Hirsch version, which was essentially a fat list of skills the Baltimore school system wanted students to master, such as identifying the main idea in a story or locating a body of water on a map—in other words, a curriculum built on the belief that skills mattered more than what kids studied. The new curriculum is far more demanding, but students rise to the challenge. "I never thought of teaching astronomy or the Roman Empire in the third grade," says teacher Pat Wolff. "Originally, I said the kids are not going to read this," adds fifth-grade teacher Regina White, whose students read abridged versions of classics such as *Julius Caesar* and the *Iliad*. "Now I know differently. Even in remedial classes, there's a lot of enthusiasm."

Test scores suggest as much. In the two years since the core-knowledge curriculum began, the proportion of fifth graders passing Maryland's state social studies test has jumped from 27 percent to 44 percent; passing grades in science have risen from 34 percent to 47 percent and in language usage from 18 percent to 49 percent. Other core-knowledge schools with large populations of disadvantaged students report similar gains.

Clearly, in these two classrooms students do much more than sit, listen, regurgitate. It is also clear, at least to me, that Regina White in the Hirsch school is no average teacher. Presumably no one teacher is identified in the Sizer excerpt (discussing *Othello* and O.J. Simpson) because classes or sections are team-taught so that all one can say is that the "team" consisted of one or all imaginative teachers. In any event, the two classrooms do not appear to be radically different from each other. Sizer is not likely to throw his hands up in disgust at Regina White's classroom, and Hirsch is not likely to indict the Sizer classroom. Although the standards they employ as well as the evidence of improvement presented are obviously different, we cannot conclude that one classroom is better than the other. Neither Hirsch nor Sizer would, I assume, say that significant increases in achievement test scores and in the number of students going to college are without *any* meaning. Using different standards and a different pedagogy, each can claim a desired outcome. How might we think about this? What questions might we ask?

Let me very briefly state several issues most relevant to standards and outcomes:

• *The "Potemkin" effect.* In the days of the Soviet Union, foreign visitors were taken to villages or other sites to show them the accomplishments of the country and its regime. Early on it was obvious that what visitors saw was, to say the least, very atypical. (Communist China has long done the same). Likewise, educational reformers will put center stage classrooms and schools in which theory and practice seem to have been successfully wedded. Rarely are we told about unsuccessful instances or the range of variation of success among schools. Readers are to be pardoned if reports about one or two schools are interpreted as justifying a conclusion about a general effect, especially if the reader is disposed favorably to the theory and pedagogy. Such a sweeping conclusion is not justified. That is certainly the case with Sizer's Coalition of Essential Schools. It is to Sizer's everlasting credit that he supported studies precisely to study this issue, and those studies

(Muncey and McQuillan, 1996) clearly demonstrate that the school in the magazine article is not typical in terms of practice and outcomes. Indeed, in his most recent book (1996) Sizer acknowledges that his efforts have not had robust effects.[4]

Hirsch has not made a similar research effort and one cannot as yet conclude from Regina White's classroom and school that Hirsch's standards-derived pedagogy and outcomes are *in general* meaningfully, intrinsically related. Hirsch's approach is now implemented in 350 schools. Can what has been reported about the Baltimore school be reported for few, or some, or most other schools? The answer to that question is crucial because Hirsch has implied (as I read him) that his no-nonsense, standards-derived pedagogy is relatively independent of teacher and school characteristics. I consider such an implication ridiculous in the extreme, although I have to say that if credible evidence confirming that general implication is forthcoming, I would have to eat crow and support Professor Hirsch for the first Nobel prize in education.

• *Lack of solid data.* If the meaning of an increase in achievement test scores is ambiguous, albeit encouraging, so is the meaning of an increase in the number of college-bound students, which is also encouraging. Both Sizer and Hirsch want students to be able to think—to acquire, digest, assimilate knowledge that allows them to use that process in independent and productive ways. Sizer is crystal clear on this point and I assume that Hirsch would not dissent. Although Sizer can present supporting anecdotal evidence— the usual "here and there" instances—neither Sizer nor Hirsch have

---

4.   I served on a team that visited and assessed three coalition high schools. There was notable variation among them, which in large measure I attribute less to the characteristics of school or teachers than to an inadequate process for monitoring the process of implementation by central staff of the coalition. To borrow terminology from Wilson (1996), discussed later in this chapter, Sizer began with a Model A; he and his colleagues learned a great deal, and I would expect that if a Model B was to be tried, the outcomes would improve. Funding sources may support a Model A, even if it is costly, but in my experience never encourage or support a Model B. You are given one time at bat and if you do not hit a home run (or a double or triple) you are through. They do not regard a single as an accomplishment. These funding sources do not take that position in regard to medical research.

presented anything resembling systematic, persuasive evidence of how students use knowledge learned in classrooms. *Is it not strange that reformers rarely (if ever) develop unbiased "tests" of how students experience, regard, and use knowledge in ways the reformers hope is the case?* Are achievement tests or entrance to college the *only* standards that are applicable or relevant? Are unbiased tests of student experience incapable of being developed and used for the very practical purpose of judging outcomes (plural) of reforms? I am reminded here of how only recently researchers have studied the way ill people view prescribed medications and how well, if at all, they follow instructions for their dosage and use. The findings are both discouraging and surprising and call into question earlier findings of the effectiveness or ineffectiveness of medications. Let us also remember that it was not always the case that drug companies and physicians were required to provide rigorous data on side effects of medication, surgery, and other invasive procedures. We are all familiar with the surgeon's claim that the surgery was successful but the patient died. In the educational arena, should we be satisfied that achievement scores increase or that more students go to college, even though there is no evidence that those students possess what Sizer calls "habits of mind"? I am not asking for a state of educational nirvana, nor do I expect that in response to any reform all or most students would meet standards of productive thinking. What I do say is that reformers should give us a basis for determining how many students show evidence that their achievement test scores are associated with productive, independent thinking. Sizer and Hirsch agree that the bulk of classrooms are unchallenging, uninteresting, unmotivating to students. Although we should find increase in scores and number of students going to college encouraging, we are not justified in concluding that those standards inform us about how students feel and think. Thomas Jefferson, Comenius, Pestalozzi, John Dewey, Maria Montessori, Rousseau, and (of course) Plato would not agree with such a conclusion. I cannot refrain from noting that contemporary women do not look fondly on the "good old days" when despite their very acceptable achievement test scores, they were judged to lack those "habits of the mind" that men with the same scores had, and that judgment, of course, was not based on evidence but on a mixture of bias, illogic, and fiat.

- *Personal style.* There are two types of physicians: those who convey a sincere sense of caring and compassion and those who may range from a ritualistic or impersonal courtesy to those who are impersonal or insensitive. The criteria for admission to medical school have little, and usually nothing, to do with those personal characteristics (Sarason, 1995a). The first category of physicians are what they are as people because that is the way they were before medical training. In the case of the second category the culture of medical training exacerbates rather than alters in any positive way the absence of interpersonal sensitivity. In the arena of psychotherapy, Strupp (1996) describes studies demonstrating that under certain conditions nonprofessionals achieve as good results as experienced professionals, which he attributes to the fact that the other practitioners and the experienced professionals were very similar in their sensitivity in interpersonal relationships.

The point of these examples, of course, is that what may be called personal style is a difference that can make a difference in interpersonal relationships irrespective of experience and espoused theory. For example, it has long been noted that very experienced psychotherapists of very different theoretical persuasions are surprisingly similar in how they are with patients, a similarity (in regard to flexibility, spontaneity, personal expression) not predictable from what their theories say about practice. That brings us back to the Hirsch and Sizer teachers described in the magazine article. They seem more similar than different, certainly in regard to imaginativeness, creativity, and even boldness. Is it unreasonable to suggest that meeting (or not meeting) high, explicit educational standards via any written curriculum is not independent of the personal characteristics of the teachers? And because teachers vary considerably in these characteristics, as do those in any other group devoted to helping people, reformers have the obligation to tell us to what degree and in what concrete ways variations in personal style among teachers affect outcomes and their meanings. When we are told that Hirsch's approach has been adopted in 350 schools and Sizer's in many more, should we attach clear meanings to those numbers in the same way that people unreflectively and unjustifiably attach meanings to achievement test scores? And, more to the present point, can we conclude that the successes are due only to the adoption of certain standards and a certain pedagogy and not at all, or minimally, to characteristics of teachers? Reformers provide us no basis to answer that question. And what about apparent failures? Are we justified in concluding that they disconfirm both the standards and the curriculum? Again, we are not provided a basis for assessing that conclusion.

In his seminal book *Redesigning Education*, Wilson (1996) points out that in designing any product, process, or program the first completed effort is regarded as Model A, with the expectation that experience with its application will determine redesign in Model B, and that the redesign process is a continuing one. Wilson gives examples of the redesign process in a variety of fields—aeronautics, agriculture, computers. Wilson correctly states that the redesign orientation and process is notable for its absence in educational reform. The redesign process is a self-correcting one, which is quite different from substituting one fad or fashion for another. The redesign process is hard, patient work that requires a no-holds-barred confrontation of problems, obstacles, mistakes, omissions. That confrontation requires observation, data, a variety of feedbacks, and a willingness (often painful in its consequences) to reexamine basic assumptions. That type of confrontation has been absent in educational reform.

In this chapter I have dealt with issues of theory and research about which I do not expect political leaders to feel at home. But I would have to agree with the criticism that in light of the large amount of money diverse parts of the federal government spend on educational research, political leaders bear ultimate responsibility for the direction and relevance of that research. And, a critic can rightly note, if government-sponsored research is to be a basis for political policymaking actions, that research should—some would say must—be carried out with real children, with real teachers in real classrooms in real schools. Furthermore, and crucially, that critic could point out that the failures of the reform movement have been to a significant degree attributable to the failure of the reformers to design and conduct their action-research— which is what an intervention is—so as to demonstrate that their results are persuasively convincing of their theory and that those results are not attainable or explainable by other theories. And by "persuasively convincing" neither the critic nor I are asking for final, once-and-for-all answers. Encouraging examples of what I mean are the work of Slavin and others (1996) on the Success For All program, that of Pinnell and others (1994) on the efficacy of Marie Clay's Reading Recovery program, and Cowen's (1996) three-plus decades of work with his Primary Mental Health Project. You can read their publications and still have questions—but you cannot, at least I cannot, deny that their guiding ideas have a high degree of demonstrable validity. You cannot say that about Hirsch, Sizer, and others who have attempted to change schools qua schools, not this or that part of schooling as a process.

The thrust of what I have said in this book and elsewhere can be put in several brief statements:

• *Classrooms.* No one is opposed to productive learning and the contexts in which that kind of learning is possible. Nevertheless, there has been a surprising lack of discussion, agreement, and research about the criteria by which one determines whether a classroom context meets those criteria.

• *Students.* There has been even less discussion and research about the criteria for determining whether students have acquired, assimilated, and utilized the cognitive characteristics that are the goals of a context for productive learning. Even so, no one claims that the bulk of classrooms meet any of those criteria. And no one has demonstrated that achievement test scores are a valid basis for concluding that the criteria have been met.

• *Schools.* The major efforts to reform schools have been designed and implemented in ways that do not allow us to explain their failures or their occasional successes; we are left with troubling questions and mysteries, giving us no basis for choosing among these efforts, leaving us in the position we frequently find ourselves in at the supermarket: Is this can of sardines healthier for us than that one; is this a better brand of beans than that one?

As luck would have it, as I was writing this chapter I received an invitation from the American Psychological Association to participate in a meeting about what psychology can contribute to school learning and change. My first reaction was one of surprise because although learning has been one of the major foci of study from the earliest days of American psychology, the profession had previously for all practical purposes shown no interest in learning in schools. If you examine the thousands of articles and books written by psychologists about the nature of human learning, you will find precious little on learning in school. This is not to say that little was learned about learning, because that is not the case. A great deal has been learned. But the significance and applicability of what was learned for the classroom was of no interest, although that was precisely what Dewey advocated in his 1899 presidential address to the American Psychological Association. So, when I got the invitation I was surprised. Why, finally, *now*? The general answer, of course, is that some psychologists believe that not only does psychology have something to contribute but that it should bring that knowledge to the attention of those who make policy in regard to education—that is, bring it to the attention of political leaders so that they will have a more secure basis for policy and research about school change. I have reason to believe that those who are seeking to arrange the meeting view governmental policy and research as near-total disasters, in part, and only in part, because (in my terms) the nature of the differences between productive and unproductive learning (and their contexts) have never been center stage.

My first reaction of surprise was replaced by a question: Why is it that political leadership has never seen fit to convene a commission to answer these three questions:

- What has been learned, and with what degree of substantiation, about the differences between productive and unproductive learning and thinking?
- What do we know, and with what degree of substantiation, about contexts that elicit and support productive thinking?
- To what extent do classrooms reflect the conclusions arrived at in the previous questions?

The commission would have an awesome task, not one that could be done in a matter of days or months. I can understand why such a commission was not formed when the government departed from tradition in the 1950s and became a stakeholder in school improvement and change. But should not one have expected, as the years passed and the desired outcomes were nowhere in evidence, that such a commission would have been formed? Such bodies were created to study similar questions about mental health, smoking, alcoholism, pollution, and more. In regard to schooling, no one, expert or not, educated or not, rich or poor, is ever in doubt that the nature and processes of learning are at the heart of schooling. So when it becomes impossible to ignore that that heart is not performing well, should we not ask what do we know about that heart? Please note that the questions posed for the commission are relatively specific and concrete. It is not being asked to come up with a program for reform. What we want to know is the state of our knowledge about human learning and the relationship of that to learning in school. It is conceivable that in regard to the first two questions the commission might conclude that clear answers are not scientifically justified at this time. I doubt that, but in that event I would expect that we would have some basis for what should be done to get justifiable answers, in which case let us say out loud that we have been and currently are flying blind.

It has long been the practice in Washington that when faced with a social problem that is divisive and has been intractable, the political leaders appoint a commission, as often as a holding action as to acquire data for different policy options. Schooling has become a divisive and intractable problem. But I am not calling for a commission such as President Reagan created, a commission whose report was as inkblottish as its charge, a report in which each recommendation lacked anything resembling a credible foundation. There *is* a difference between opinion and evidence. We didn't get to the moon, split the atom, develop effective vaccines on the basis of opinion. None of these rival in difficulty what is involved in changing traditional human institutions. In the realm of human affairs and its major problems we never can have final solutions. That in no way absolves us of the obligation to base our efforts on the most credible evidence available to us. We will always fall short of the mark. That is no sin. What is sinful is not knowing what the mark is, which is the case with school change.

Chapter Six

The Content and Style of Teaching

In the *New York Times* for December 29, 1996, Albert Shanker's column is titled "Remembering Teachers."[1] In that column he discusses a book about famous people (living or dead) who in their memoirs had singled out a teacher who had dramatically affected their lives. Shanker says, "In almost every case, these favorite teachers were in love with their subject, and, because attaining great knowledge and the skill to deploy it requires discipline, they also demanded hard work of their students." Shanker emphasizes that these teachers not only loved what they taught but also communicated that love to students.

That there were and are such teachers is unquestionable. Shanker then goes on to say that it is unfortunate that within the educational community there is a "prejudice against content. Prospective teachers are often indoctrinated with the idea that they should 'teach the student, not the subject.' That means focusing on the process of learning—on 'problem solving', 'higher order thinking skills' and 'critical thinking' rather than American history, or *Macbeth,* or W.E.B. DuBois." How, Shanker asks, can you teach these processes without content?

Shanker's column begs far more questions than it purports to answer. For example, let us assume there is a kernel of truth to his criticism of a prejudice against content. When and why did that

---

1. As I noted in the previous chapter, Albert Shanker died in February 1997; see my remembrances of him in the preface of this book.

prejudice get articulated in the post–World War II educational reform movement? The brief answer is that in the 1950s a mounting criticism of schools began on two grounds. The first was that classroom learning required drill, rote memory, and regurgitation. The second was that the content or subject matter (the curriculum) was blatantly narrow, misleading, or (depending on the subject matter) scientifically or historically wrong or outmoded—that is, it was less a sample of a particular subject matter than it was a mockery of it. The third was that subject matter was not only center stage— nothing else mattered—but it was taught in ways that extinguished whatever love of learning students had when they started school. There was really a fourth reason: whatever degree of love teachers had for their subject matter rarely got communicated to students.

It is not playing fast and loose with history to say that the advocates and developers of curriculum reform were indicting *impoverished* content and *impoverished* preparatory programs for teachers, a combination that over the decades had made for and sustained boring and stultifying classrooms. Indeed, the aim of the curriculum reformers was not only to broaden and deepen the presentation of content but also to suggest ways that would elicit the interest and curiosity of students—that is, stimulate them to think about subject matter and not be satisfied with simply being able to regurgitate it, to understand that there is not one and only one way to think about and react to something as complicated as this or that subject matter.

The curriculum reformers of the 1950s and 1960s would not have disagreed with Shanker's statement that you cannot think without content (anywhere, anytime) but they would have reminded him that in and of itself content is no guarantor of productive thinking. Content is no silver bullet. That is precisely the point of the movie *Mr. Holland's Opus,* a movie about which Shanker had earlier written so approvingly. Mr. Holland loved, truly loved, the subject matter he taught but his students reacted with apathy, sarcasm, and thinly veiled hostility; as a result Mr. Holland reacted to his students with disdain. It was not until he achieved insight about how his psychology and pedagogy were counterproductive that he could communicate his love of subject matter to his students—he had to begin to love his students the way he did his subject before he could reach them.

Why did the curriculum reforms fail? The answer is too complex to be taken up here. I have discussed this in earlier publications in some detail (Sarason, 1996a) and I can assure the reader that the answer is indeed complex. What is relevant for my present purposes is that part of the answer that derives from personal experience. I (and my late wife) personally observed and studied the process by which the new curricula were introduced into schools. Let me briefly and chronologically describe what we observed:

The decision to introduce the new curricula was made by boards of education and school administrators. Teachers played no role in the decision and they greeted the decision with a noticeable lack of enthusiasm. If the new curriculum was not presented to the teachers as the best thing since sliced bread, it came close to that.

Because the new curricula (the new math, new physics, new biology, new social studies) would be unfamiliar to teachers and require changes in their attitudes, knowledge, and pedagogy, they participated in workshops. These workshops were of two to five days in duration.

It was blatantly obvious during the workshops that teachers were having a great deal of difficulty comprehending the rationale and methods of the new curricula. The feelings of teachers varied from anxiety to unexpressed or muted hostility to apathy and psychological withdrawal. In only a few of the workshops did somewhat more than a handful of teachers ask questions—and even they were not satisfied by the answers. By the end of a workshop teachers seemed to be unanimous in the feeling that the workshops were too brief, too pressured, and unsatisfying.

It was not until we had completed our observations that we saw something that should have been obvious earlier: teachers had been put in a situation in which they were required to *unlearn* their previous ways of thinking and teaching and to learn new, unfamiliar knowledge and methods. Those requirements under the best of conditions are difficult both to experience and meet. Under the conditions of the workshops those requirements were invitations to disaster.

Now for the clincher. *Those who conducted the workshops approached the teachers in exactly the same way that Mr. Holland approached his students, which was the same way the teachers in the workshop taught their students.* That is to say, those who conducted the workshops riveted so on the content they wished to get across that they were totally insensitive to the plight and reactions of the teachers; they loved the new subject matter, they had mastered it, they tried sincerely and valiantly to communicate that love, but, again like Mr. Holland, they were puzzled and dismayed by the difficulties teachers were experiencing. The workshops were instances of contexts of unproductive learning.

You can criticize the curriculum reformers for a number of mistakes but you cannot impugn their aim both to broaden and deepen subject matter. Like Shanker, they saw a crying need for a curriculum that would be challenging and interesting to students—but not at the expense of a watered-down subject matter. They were quite aware that communicating that curriculum in an appropriate way could only be done by teachers who knew and loved their subject matter, and yet in private conversation with me the reformers were vehemently critical of preparatory programs that, to use Shanker's verb, "indoctrinated" teachers with a pedagogy that would defeat the purposes of *any* curriculum purporting or deserving of being called educational or intellectually respectable. The irony, of course, is that the reformers employed the very pedagogy they were criticizing—they riveted on subject matter, unaware that they were ignoring their own dictum of starting where the students are, understanding where they are coming from, and using that knowledge to hook the students and to steer or guide them so as to enlarge their understanding and foster attitudes toward new facets of the subject matter they needed to assimilate and productively utilize.

What I found most surprising and dispiriting in Shanker's comments is his disdain for the maxim "you teach children, not subject matter," a maxim encapsulating John Dewey's conception of learning in the classroom. To suggest, as Shanker does, that the maxim is a downgrading of the importance of subject matter is sheer nonsense. What Dewey said over and over again is that content is too important for personal, social, and vocational purposes to be introduced and taught in a way that ignored where the learner is coming from, where he or she is starting, and the bedrock importance of relating subject matter to his or her experience, outlook, attitudes, and questions. To put it bluntly: You are not teaching stones, machines, or automatons but thinking, feeling human beings about whom you know for certain that each possesses a distinctive individuality that will be crucial in determining the degree and quality of understanding and utilization of subject matter. The artistry of teaching is in arranging a marriage between individuality and subject matter. When we say "you teach children, not subject matter," we seek to prevent a divorce between two partners who truly need each other. The teacher presides over that marriage; the teacher does not arrange and preside over a shotgun wedding where one party ends up bored, unmotivated, unthinking, a passive conformer for whom subject matter has no generalizing personal and intellectual challenge and consequence. Dewey compared the modal teacher of his day to an army commander who, of course, could not be less interested in how recruits thought and felt, the order of the day being pay attention, do as I say, don't ask questions, and I will give you a good rating.

Recently the board of education of the city of Hartford publicly circulated its new standards for each grade level. Here are the expectations for the first three grades in regard to science.

Grade 1

- Apply the scientific process of observing, recording, sorting, classifying, and measuring
- Understand the ways some things change
- Recognize naturally occurring cycles

Grade 2

- Apply the scientific process of observing, recording, sorting, classifying, and measuring
- Analyze changes in the environment
- Recognize cycles and patterns found in nature

Grade 3

- Apply the scientific process of observing, recording, classifying, measuring, hypothesizing, analyzing, and evaluating data
- Recognize changes caused by energy and weather

- Analyze the interdependence among plants, animals, and humans

I find little to criticize in those expectations. However, preceding the expectations for *each* of the grade levels are the italicized words *The Student Will*. For whom are those semi-intimidating words intended? Clearly, they contain a message to teachers: "We expect that you *will* get your students to meet these standards." The problems of the Hartford schools have been reported in the mass media. (Those schools have been and still are at the very bottom of Connecticut's schools on achievement tests.) The new standards are intended to raise scores on these tests and, of course, that will require teachers to concentrate even more on subject matter. As best as I can determine from my sources on the scene, concentrating is precisely what Hartford teachers say they have been doing and they regard the new standards as saying in different words what has long been the case. So why have students learned so little? Why should one expect that they *will* do better in the future? The answer to the first question is that classrooms in Hartford lack almost all of the features of contexts of productive learning, an answer that is no less relevant to almost all schools in our urban areas. The answer to the second question is that I expect the future of the Hartford schools will be a carbon copy of the present because there is a divorce between subject matter and why and how children learn. The teacher is the bridge between subject matter and student will and motivation. It is far too often the case that the bridge the teacher builds allows only one-way traffic, from teacher to student. That kind of bridge defines unproductive learning, as Mr. Holland found out.

Shanker began his column by extolling some unusual teachers who had influenced the lives of some people who had become famous. Having been mystified over the past two years by Shanker's emphasis on the power of elevated standards to improve educational outcomes, I read the beginning section of his column with trepidation. Was he going to conclude that the teachers he described at the outset are a representative sample of teachers in general, a conclusion as unwarranted as his emphasis on the magical-psychological power of elevated standards? For all practical purposes he does just that in the final paragraph. Teachers, he says, "are skilled in techniques of what we now call class-room management. They are sensitive to who their students are and know what kinds of approaches will help the youngsters learn." That is a clear example of wish fulfillment, a confusion between fact and fiction.

In September 1996, the National Commission on Teaching and America's Future published its report. The commission consisted of twenty-seven members, all but a handful of whom spend their days in one or another role directly relevant to school improvement. To call them public school educators is to state the obvious. The executive director was Linda Darling-Hammond of Teachers College, Columbia University, one of the most thoughtful, non-polemical, and productive contributors in matters relating to teaching. In my experience this report puts 99 percent of comparable educational reports to shame because of its candor, scope, and specificity. I urge the reader to read and ponder its contents. Here is an excerpt from the report:

> The bad news [about innovative programs] is that these efforts are not the norm in education—nor are they systematically incorporated into the education system. What we find, instead, is a promising innovation here, a new practice there, but only rarely are they connected to each other. At the same time, the relentless need for teachers means that many states and districts continue to ignore entry standards for teachers, quietly reneging on their obligations to students and the rhetorical commitments they have made to parents.
>
> What is required is a great national crusade united behind the position that competent teaching is a new student right. We must understand that if this nation is to prepare all of its children for the challenges of the 21st century, teaching must be able to recruit and retain able, well-prepared teachers for *all* classrooms. These entrants must be equipped with the knowledge, skills, and dispositions that will enable them to succeed with *all* students. And, *all* of their workplaces must offer them the support they need to develop and grow as professionals in a lifelong career [p. 57].

It is hard—I would say impossible—to read this report and not to conclude that the preparation of teachers is, generally speaking, in a sorry state, a conclusion I have discussed in two earlier books (Sarason, 1993a; Sarason, Davidson, and Blatt, 1986). Granted, in the past few years a very small number of programs have done well, and the report recognizes this. But as the excerpt states, those instances are very far from being a norm. As I have repeatedly said, an innovation here and an innovation there do not constitute a trend. It is to the credit of the person or persons who wrote the report, as well as to the twenty-seven commission members who approved it, that it makes no bones about how far we have to go and how long it will take before we see a general improvement in the quality of teaching even if the recommendations in the report are taken seriously.

The irony is that Shanker was a member of the commission. He did not write a dissenting report; he signed off on this one. Yet the report flatly contradicts the generalizations he makes about America's teachers.

In all the years Shanker has been writing his column I can recall no instance where he directly (or for that matter, indirectly) discussed, analyzed, and evaluated preparatory programs. I can understand that omission. After all, his constituency consists of teachers who would not warmly greet anything their president said that suggested teachers were ill prepared for their role. In addition, a significant number of the faculty of college preparatory programs are also members of his union. You do not bite the hand that feeds you. Shanker is a very knowledgeable, thoughtful, politically astute person. That he approved of the commission report is to his credit. That he then wrote a column at variance (an understatement) with that report is not to his credit. I think I am correct in saying that his column was read by many more people than will read the commission report. Those who will read the report will be a relatively small segment of the educational community. Those who read his column are not small in number and they include members of the political establishment, to many of whom Shanker has easy access. What is discouraging is that after reading his column political leaders and the general public will conclude that the preparation of teachers is not a serious problem.

The commission report is remarkable in numerous ways but here I wish only to mention two of them. The first is that it is not a polemic against or an indictment of teachers. On the contrary, it makes clear that the inadequacies of many teachers are a consequence of a *system* made up of the practices and attitudes of colleges and universities; school cultures uncongenial to and even destructive of contexts of productive learning both for teachers and students; boards of education and school administrators who tolerate incompetence, give lip service (if that) to professional development, do little or nothing to upgrade quality of teaching or the enforcement of standards, and do not *seek* teachers of demonstrated competence and quality; political leaders who do not comprehend the seriousness of the situation, especially in our cities, and lack the will to start to do what needs to be done; a public (not only parents) that no part of the system attempts to make more knowledgeable and a force for change. Consider the following in the commission report:

By the standards of other professions and of teacher education in other countries, U.S. teacher education has historically been thin, uneven, and poorly financed. Although some schools of education provide high-quality preparation, others are treated as "cash cows" by their universities, bringing in revenues that are spent on the education of doctors, lawyers, and accountants rather than on their own students. As a result, teachers do not always have adequate disciplinary preparation in the fields they teach or adequate knowledge and supervised practice to enable them to use effective teaching strategies.

Moreover, teacher recruitment is ad hoc; hiring and tenure decisions are often disconnected from any clear vision of quality teaching; beginning teacher mentoring and professional development for experienced teachers are the first things eliminated in budget cuts. Working in isolation with few chances to update their skills, teachers are deprived of knowledge that would allow them to succeed at much higher levels. Meanwhile, most education dollars are spent on staff and activities other than classroom teaching.

But our schools' most closely held secret amounts to a great national shame: Without telling parents they are doing so, many districts hire unqualified people as "teachers" and assign them full responsibility for children. More than 12 percent of all newly hired "teachers" enter without any training at all and another 14 percent enter without having fully met state standards. Although no state will allow a person to fix plumbing, guard swimming pools, style hair, write wills, design a building, or practice medicine without completing training and passing an examination, more than

40 states allow school districts to hire teachers on emergency licenses who have not met these basic requirements. States pay more attention to the qualifications of veterinarians treating the nation's cats and dogs than to those of teachers educating the nation's children and youth [National Commission on Teaching and America's Future, 1996, p. 15].

The second remarkable feature of the report is captured in an excerpt from a brief article by a teacher, Cynthia Ellwood, in Milwaukee. I have in earlier pages used such terms and phrases as productive learning, starting with where the learner is, hooking the learner, and helping him or her to make connections between personal experience and new knowledge. Ellwood puts into words what previous reports ignored or glossed over.

At the very core of teaching is the task of helping students make connections between what they already understand and the new concepts, information, or skills [we want them to learn]. Scientists of the human mind tell us we can remember very few totally separate items at once, and all learning is a process of somehow associating new information with old. So this is my job as a teacher: to help students make connections. And to do that, I need to have a pretty good picture of what their understandings are—or I need a way to probe those understandings.

At any moment, I have to decide whether to present information or stand back and let a student discover it. I have to know when and how to encourage, compel, accept, judge, nurture, admonish, humor, provoke, and inspire 30 individuals. Now if I am teaching your son or daughter, you undoubtedly hope that I understand your child well enough to make those decisions—so often spontaneous ones—wisely. And if I really understand your kid, if I can see into his soul a bit, or if I can figure out how his mind works when he's wrestling with a particular concept or skill, or if I can find a way to make him passionately interested in what I teach, I just might be able to inspire him to real heights. But if I don't understand, I can damage your child. I can turn him off, or set him back, or crush his feelings, or stifle his opportunities.

If I as one teacher fail to reach, nurture, and inspire your son or daughter, it's probably not the end of the world; a child can probably recover from this single experience. But if entire educational systems repeatedly misjudge or work ineffectively with certain children—we have a problem of national dimensions [National Commission on Teaching and America's Future, 1996, p. 11].

We do have a problem of national dimensions! You can build new schools, change curricula, elevate standards, lengthen the school day and year, and more, but if that problem of national dimensions is not squarely faced, the one thing you can give odds and bet on is that not long after the twenty-first century begins another commission will issue a report like the one Darling-Hammond so admirably directed.

Will the president read the report? My answer to that question is given in the next chapter.

Chapter Seven

Charter Schools and the Creation of Settings

I assume that no one would say that the plight of our schools should be blamed on the president and others in high political office, just as no one would say they caused the diverse aspects of environmental pollution. But in those and comparable instances we have four expectations: our officials will act, we will be provided with criteria by which to judge the consequences of those actions, if those actions and consequences are demonstrably ineffective we will be so informed, and we will be informed about why new actions will not be based on ideas and assumptions undergirding previous actions. In regard to public schooling, political leadership has to be regarded as having failed. Failure is no secular sin unless the failure is the most recent example of a long-standing pattern of failure, a pattern in which little or nothing has been learned from experience, a kind of repetition compulsion.

It is, of course, the case that the problem of school change is an enormously complicated one (an understatement); it does not have a solution in the sense that four divided by two has a solution. Nor is it a problem for which we can set target dates for the proclamation of victory. Indeed, the most obvious, egregious, inexcusable mistake of past and current actions is setting target dates that expose the depths of ignorance of those who set those dates. (It is like saying that the more than forty wars, civil or otherwise, currently taking place on this planet will cease by the year 2000.) The time perspective you adopt is based on the comprehensiveness and plausibility of your diagnosis, and in the case of educational change

anyone whose diagnosis permits the setting of target dates is ignorant, or a fool, or both—however well-intentioned the person is.
That, I know, sounds harsh but not to anyone who knows the history of educational reform of the past fifty years. As someone once
said, "Tell me the problem with which a person is confronted, tell
me the time perspective he or she is adopting, and I will tell you
the degree to which the person is in touch with the social realities."

Imagine you are in a meeting with other educators and in
walks a stranger who says, "I heard that a group of educators was
meeting here and I decided to come in because I have a question
to which I would like an answer. I have to be frank and say that I
have long been of the opinion that educators have a genius for
making simple problems very complex. My question is this: Why
can't you teach a child to read, if not in a day, then in a month?
How do you justify making a prolonged big deal about learning to
read?" Being polite, you do not ask the person to leave the room
and get psychological help. You would explain why it would take
you a good part of a day just to outline all the factors and processes
that set the stage for a child to want and to be ready to begin to
read—the growth and vicissitudes of sensory-motor, linguistic, cognitive, and affective development; the role of books and reading
in the family context; the nurturing of a child's curiosity and need
for the feeling of competence; and more, much more. Even assuming that the child is ready to learn to read, the classroom context
is not a one-on-one situation. Still, there are individual differences
that have to be discerned, respected, and adapted to, and not every
child can or should be taught in the same way. From the standpoint of the child, learning to discriminate among written letters
and words is not a narrow technical process; it is one that requires
an integration of cognitive, motivational, visual factors that mature
over time, an integration that is occurring in all spheres of the
child's life and varies in rate and consequences among children.
Learning to read does not guarantee that comprehension of written words and sentences has kept pace. Learning to read and comprehend is complicated both for teacher and child. And when it is
the case that the classroom is the only place a child experiences
reading, learning to read is even more difficult and complicated.

The point here is that the difference in time perspective between
the stranger and you inheres in wildly different conceptions of the

nature of child development and, therefore, what children modally are, become, and can learn—and when. To the stranger, teaching the child to read should in principle be no more difficult or time-consuming than following a recipe. To you, learning to read is like learning to teach: It ain't easy!

I would argue on historical grounds that teaching children to read is a piece of cake compared with trying to change schools. In principle they are identical in that both require a knowledge of the nature and purposes of the host organism that is the object of change. When political leaders set target dates for when schools will change and children will learn, they have to be criticized for a degree of ignorance similar to that of the stranger I described earlier. But unrealistic time perspective is but one symptom of the misunderstanding of the complexity of educational reform. Let us turn to what is the most recent proposal for reform that national and state political leaders have embraced. I refer to charter schools.

Readers of this book have heard about charter schools—those explicit, deliberate attempts on the part of state political leadership to create schools that will be relatively independent of existing school systems. (They are not attempts indigenous to the educational community.) The charter school movement rests on the diagnosis that existing school systems are inimical and intractable to innovating and achieving improved educational outcomes. Almost every state has passed enabling legislation. In 1996 the Connecticut legislature created twenty-four such charter schools. In his first press conference after his reelection (January 1997) President Clinton called for a tripling of the number of charter schools funded through states with federal funds. It is hard to exaggerate the importance of the charter school; it is the first attempt to do something radical about school reform. It rests on one assumption and one hope. The assumption—which is never verbalized but is implicit—is that schools and school systems are or may be unrescuable. The hope is, of course, that the charter school will provide instructive data to those responsible for educational policy. Since charter schools will receive the same per capita support as traditional schools (or slightly more), if they are successful (more productive of desirable outcomes), the economic implications are, to say the least, enormous.

Several questions have to be asked. The first question stems from the fact that in each state each of the charter schools is for all practical purposes on its own—that is, it will determine how it will use its fiscal and human resources to achieve the purposes it stated in its application for special status. The first question is: What will be the relationship among these schools embarked on uncharted seas? I am familiar with the legislation and implementation in several states. The fact is that nothing is said or being done about how these schools can be of help to each other. As I pointed out a quarter of a century ago (Sarason, 1972), the creation of a new setting brings in its wake several *predictable* problems.[1] These problems include the following:

- The creators almost always underestimate the complexity of creating a new setting. It is the opposite of an easy, smooth, untroubled process.
- They also underestimate the time factor, an underestimation that too frequently pressures them to make compromises and to gloss or seal over conceptual and interpersonal problems that will later come to haunt them.
- Imbued as they are with enthusiasm about being able to create a new setting, the creators cannot deal with the fact that resources are always limited, with the result that when reality confronts them with that brute fact, they are not prepared to deal with it.
- If anything is predictable about creating a new setting, it is that unpredictable problems will be encountered—for example, something happens to the leader, the inadequacies of this or that staff member become manifest, outside opposition or criticism appears.

---

1.   In *The Creation of Settings and the Future Societies* (1972), I define a new setting as one where two or more people get together in new and sustained relationships to achieve agreed-upon goals. Just as when the original Head Start legislation meant that hundreds of new settings would be created, so does the charter school legislation mean that several hundred new settings will be created in the next year or so, and many more will follow, as fashion plays its accustomed, compelling role. In an enlarged edition of the book mentioned above (Sarason, forthcoming), several of the new chapters go into detail about why I predict charter schools, generally speaking, will fall short of the mark.

In brief, these encapsulated charter schools will experience similar kinds of problems, however different their written application, mode of organization, and pedagogy may be. It is also predictable that some of these schools will cope more effectively with these issues than others. *It is inconceivable that these schools have nothing to give or take from each other.* From my perspective that is not only a glimpse of the obvious but the beginning step in what I regard as a crucial goal: to define and utilize existing resources so that they are mutually and productively enlarged and *exchanged*. I italicized the word *exchanged* because it implies a degree of mutual understanding and knowledge that makes for a discernible increase in the productive use of existing resources. Someone said that money is a necessary means of exchange among strangers. But when money is absent or realistically not in the picture, one is still left with the power of an informal connectedness that makes for mutual understanding and a willing exchange of resources. Unfortunately, such connectedness does not exist among charter schools. Each has the assets and deficits of a rampant, rugged individualism.

How should we think about the enthusiasm and speed with which political leaders have embraced charter schools? For someone like me, the good news about charter schools is that they direct our attention to a system of education and its governance that I regard as fatally flawed (Sarason, 1997). The bad news is that for all practical purposes we will never know why a charter school failed or why it achieved whatever success it publicly claims. Political leaders have been inexcusably irresponsible in describing charter schools as if the process by which they come into existence and develop is as clear as the rationale for the autonomy they seek and are granted. These leaders convey the impression that a charter school is one that has written a worthy, supportable charter and that what follows is a kind of organizational engineering. Period. That is demonstrable, mischievous nonsense. To create and sustain a new setting that will achieve most of its stated purposes is very complicated, which is why the divorce rate is so high, and why a large percentage of new businesses fail outright or miss their mark to a glaring extent.

What is it that permits political leaders initially to support creating a very small number of charter schools and, then, in short order—*before anything is known about the obstacle course such schools confront*—to call for a dramatic increase in their numbers? One part of the answer is that the phrase "charter school" not only sounds refreshingly innovative, suggesting an unleashing of creative ideas and energies, an extraction of the pure from the impure, but those characteristics are considered as self-evident truths guaranteeing that these schools will achieve these stated purposes. Unlike their approach to other areas, where governments adopt a new initiative and then study and evaluate real-life instances as carefully as possible, political leaders have talked themselves and the public into believing that if charter schools could be manufactured in great numbers, we would have taken a giant step on the way to improving our public schools. But we know that creating a charter school is conceptually, interpersonally, and organizationally a can of worms; that charter schools should be expected to go from Model A to Model B to Model C depending on how and what is learned from internal and external pressures and mistakes; that unless these schools have forums and processes for self-correction their rate of failure will be very high. Is the creation of charter schools, unlike other instances of the creation of settings, exempt from what we know about the creation of settings? Do we have to be subjected to yet another instance of an educational innovation the implementation of which is a catalogue of errors of omission and commission?

As I said earlier, I regard the call for charter schools to be indicative of the beginning of an awareness among political leaders that our educational system is the problem and that it is incapable of generating a solution. It deserves emphasis that charter schools are expected to be (whether they will be or not is another story) exempt from all those system characteristics that make schools the stifling, infantilizing, unchallenging places most of them are. It is precisely because I regard the potentialities of charter schools so highly that I find it difficult to be other than damning of political leaders who fail to apply to education what they know or do to some degree in other arenas of societal problems. Why is there no serious effort to evaluate the new initiative so as to have a basis for spending large sums of money to spread those aspects of it that demonstrate credible evidence of the desired effects?

Or is it that political leaders do not want to be perceived as going too slowly about an innovation that they (the political leaders) have gone on record as stating is the best and newest solution we possess? They become captive of their own rhetoric, they are gratified by the public's positive response to the charter school idea, and their initially modest initiative begins to become a movement or crusade. It is a process of self-congratulation and of the appearance of leadership that ignores the distinctions between good intentions and demonstrated outcomes. It is also a process with a long and sorry history in educational reform.

Richard Darman was director of the Office of Management and Budget in President Bush's administration. In the *New York Times Magazine* for December 1, 1996, there is an article by him with the arresting title "Riverboat Gambling with Government." The equally arresting subtitle is "The scandal is not that Washington has failed to pursue bold domestic visions. The scandal is that Washington rolls the dice before it knows what it is doing." If you read this concise, to-the-point article with charter schools and vouchers in mind, you will understand why it takes a denial of the past and the adoption of the rosiest of views of the future to believe that charter schools and vouchers will "of course" transform our educational ills from the category of intractable to that of tractable.

Darman's critique focuses on President Clinton and the Washington scene. The fact is that in regard to charter schools and vouchers the initiative was that of some governors. That fact is important because Darman rightly criticizes our recent presidents (not only Clinton) for what he calls "policy corruption."

> The Government also sponsored experiments ranging from loosely structured model cities to more systematic trials of particular policy ideas. A multi-city test of housing allowances was designed to examine effects on housing demand and supply. In New Jersey, an ambitious test of welfare reform examined work incentives and the negative income tax. Other experiments were structured to test innovative approaches to remedial education, job training, health insurance and school choice. Importantly, these experiments were designed to test behavior and results outside of the ivory tower, at substantial scale, in the real world.
>
> Unfortunately, however, most of these experimental efforts were abandoned before they could deliver—often before they were

fully financed. Given the enormous stakes, one might well wonder why. Why have we not organized a sustained effort to learn?

However, compared with governors who have jumped on the bandwagon of vouchers and charter schools, one is tempted to describe our recent presidents as sophisticated scientists and researchers possessed of such probity and knowledge as to prevent them from overselling interested ideas and programs. In the corridors of power in Washington, terms like research and evaluation may not be the rage but neither are they odious in their implications. In our state capitals, however, especially in regard to matters educational, a Martian could spend months seeing and hearing legislators and governors go about their business and never realize that there are words like research and evaluation in the English language. So when Connecticut's governor took pride in the passage of the charter school legislation, he did not tell the public that the legislation provided no provision or funds for maximizing what can be learned from the first generation of charter schools and incorporating that learning into a second generation of charter schools.

I should hasten to say that we have no ready-made way or program for designing and evaluating charter schools. How you evaluate depends on how well you understand the phenomena and vicissitudes of the process of creating and sustaining a charter school. As I pointed out in *The Creation of Settings* (1972), a new setting can be studied prospectively or retrospectively, and each approach is beset with thorny problems. But of one thing my experience has convinced me: the more data obtained relevant to the earliest phases of setting creation, the more likely it is that one can determine the sources of the degree of failure and success of the new setting. A charter school is a challenge not only to its creators but also to the researcher-evaluator. To oversimplify the issues involved is to make it likely that the most radical—and, in my opinion, necessary—challenge to the existing educational system will be one from which we will learn little or nothing or, worse yet, come to unjustified conclusions.

The federal Department of Education has contracted with a policy analysis and research firm to study and evaluate charter schools. I was able to obtain a one-and-a-third page "study overview" of the proposed project. Nothing in that document leads me to believe that the four-year study will provide anything resembling adequate data to address the questions I have raised. For example, in the first year—which will presumably be *after* the first year of the schools' existence—data will consist of school and student characteristics obtained *through a telephone survey.*

After this book was in production, a study by Abby Weiss (1997) of the Institute for Responsive Education at Northeastern University in Boston was made available to me. Through a grant from the William Casper Memorial Fund, she studied five charter schools in Massachusetts that had been in existence for one year or somewhat more. Teams of two to three researchers spent one day at each school, visiting classes and governance group meetings, touring the facilities, interviewing principals, founders, teachers, parents, and students, and conducting focus groups of students, parents, and teachers. They visited two urban schools and three suburban, all within one and one-half hours of Boston. The five schools represent different grade spans: kindergarten through fifth grade, kindergarten through eighth grade, fifth through eight grade, sixth through eighth grade, and seventh through ninth grade.

Weiss's report is relatively brief and her final conclusions and recommendations fairly mirror what she presented earlier in her report. I am indebted to the Institute for permission to quote that entire section.

Conclusions and Recommendations

From our interviews, focus groups, and classroom observations, we learned that, in general, all of the charter school stake holders are very pleased with their experiences. Students are overwhelmingly positive when describing their charter schools. Parents are happy with charter schools both because they see that their children are interested and engaged in school, and because they themselves feel connected and needed. Teachers have a high degree of satisfaction, as do their principals, because of the freedom the charter school experience gives them and the ability to be flexible in meeting their students' needs. Moreover, the high level of collaboration and team work contributes to their contentment.

On the other hand, there are significant barriers preventing charter schools from fully realizing their mission. These barriers stem from significant organizational development issues which are impeding their progress, in many cases, on educational issues. These organizational development issues—governance, lack of sufficient time, public relations—are the types of problems which would face any new organization, but the difficulty in the charter schools is that these issues must be addressed while also educating students. Financial issues are important barriers to principals in their second year of operation. Ongoing financial planning is a major issue; however, this is mostly in the context of accommodating an ever-expanding student population. Finances were critical in the planning phases, when facilities were initially being sought and other start-up costs were mounting. Finances will again be a critical issue as schools need to seek larger, more appropriate, and more permanent facilities.

In other types of schools—both public and independent—there are associations and other organizations and support systems which help schools meet some of these needs. For example, private schools are members of state and national associations which provide access to research and assistance. Public schools have local districts and states to help them manage their organizational needs. Of course, in public schools, these supports come with the bureaucracy that charter schools are trying to avoid. However, without any supports, charter schools are at a distinct disadvantage.

Charter schools will not be able to thrive without assistance in meeting these organizational and educational needs. From our conversations with charter school staff and parents, we can conclude that charter schools need technical assistance and the eyes of an outsider to help them address their concerns. In several instances, when we left a school, teachers and principals asked us for our outsider's perspective on their school. Schools are hungry for feedback and for assistance, but there is as yet no structure or budget in place for such support. Schools also need to be involved in an ongoing process to help them determine their school improvement priorities, to address these priorities, and to document their successes and effects on their public school counterparts.

There are different ways these needs could be met. First, charter schools could agree to form their own voluntary associations in which a third party would coordinate their efforts, inform charter schools of other schools which are facing similar issues, provide technical assistance, and generally minimize the current level of isolation felt among charter schools. Only those schools that were interested would participate, and, unlike the current district model, charter schools would dictate the level and type of supports they would receive from this affiliation. In time, this type of fee for service regional association project could provide a new model for organizing school districts.

Another approach would be to have a state agency undertake this role and coordinate the delivery of technical assistance to the charter schools. In Massachusetts, the state is currently coordinating the ongoing evaluation of charter schools. If the state chose to undertake the role of providing technical assistance as well as monitoring, it would be important to ensure that a school requiring a certain type of assistance or support would receive that help without fear of losing their autonomy. To prevent this from occurring, the state must have two separate teams conducting this work—one for ongoing evaluation and another for technical assistance and support.

While the autonomy these schools enjoy accounts for a great deal of satisfaction among members of the charter school community and appears to provide these schools with many exciting opportunities, it is also isolating. Without a concerted effort to draw charter schools together as a community and to provide them with needed support, the autonomy they have fought for may ultimately prove to be an insurmountable barrier.

The report makes it compellingly clear that these schools possess the hallmarks of a new setting: great hopes, enthusiasm, a sense of purpose and community. But it is no less clear that neither the state department of education nor the local planners of the charter schools envisioned or dealt with the predictable problems a new setting would encounter, not the least of which were time, limited resources, issues of governance, and clarity of criteria by which accomplishments would be judged. These schools are, Weiss says, "hungry for assistance." The point I am emphasizing is that some of the major problems for which they seek assistance could and should have been known by those who advocated and obtained enabling legislation for these charter schools, and I include here the state department of education. Put in another way, the existing governance of the educational system is incapable of initiating a radical innovation that does justice to and confronts the predictable, practical problems that innovation will encounter. Presidents, governors, legislators, commissioners of education have hailed charter school legislation with much self-serving fanfare, as if they understood what creating such schools would entail. I am in no way suggesting that we know all that we need to know about creating new settings, but I am asserting that we have learned several things. First, the educational system is allergic to a radical departure. Second, we have learned something about creating new settings. Third, any radically new educational innovation has to be regarded as a Model A to be superseded by Models B and C as experience and the self-correcting stance dictates. Fourth, the self-correcting stance is alien to those who formulate educational policy.

Each of the charter schools Weiss studied was visited for one day. Coming as that fact did at the beginning of the report, I was ready to indict Weiss and the sponsors of the study for methodological and conceptual malfeasance. By the end of reading this brief report, I was surprised that a one-day visit had identified the major, predictable problems that the charter schools had to encounter, problems I have to predict will become increasingly thorny, a prediction with which Weiss agrees in her last sentence.

Charter schools call for a longitudinal methodology and not one that depends, as Weiss's does, very largely on what participants say. What people say is, of course, very important—but so is the relationship between what they say and what they do and the factors that affect, positively or negatively, the quality and outcomes of those relationships. If the Model A version of charter schools is ever to be improved in a Model B it will have to be based on studies providing us new understandings. Given the history of educational reform, making it possible to gain those understandings is something presidents, governors, and state commissioners of education seem to be incapable of confronting. They regard charter schools as a solution in the sense that four divided by two has a solution. In the realm of human affairs there are no such solutions and the best we can do—in the tradition of the self-correcting stance—is to try systematically and dispassionately to learn from experience. It is no sin to fall short of the mark. It is sinful not to have a mark. The question is not whether charter schools will have x or y degree of success or failure. The question—it is less a question than an obligation—is to have a basis for understanding why some charter schools may achieve their goals and others will not, and to take that understanding seriously.

It was beyond my purposes to discuss in any detail the research design for studies of charter schools. But I do want to point out that there are (at least) two questions with which such studies must deal. First, *regardless of which criteria are employed in regard to outcomes, how do charter school students and personnel compare with students and personnel in the schools from which the former came?* That comparison is less difficult (but still difficult) to do in regard to students than in regard to personnel but it is crucial. This would require for each student in a charter school that there be a control student from the same school from which the charter school student came, the two being matched in ways having some degree of face validity—that is, you would try to avoid comparing apples and oranges. Charter schools are intended to demonstrate that their students will over time demonstrate attitudes, skills, and accomplishments they would have had not at all or in lesser degree if they had remained in their traditional school. A "control" methodology is obviously indicated.

I have already alluded to the second question: *How do we determine why charter schools vary in their degree of success or failure in regard to their stated goals?* The answer cannot be determined by one- or two-day visits listening to what people say. Nor can you begin to study the schools a year or more after they are in existence—that is, after the most problem-producing, future-determining stage is lost to memory and analysis. If we are ever to develop a Model B that will capitalize on the errors of omission and commission in Model A—or on the predictably few instances of exemplary outcomes—charter schools have to begin to be studied before they roll out the welcome mat for students. The "before the beginning" stage is a crucial one. Not all acorns become oak trees. Not all normal newborns become untroubled, competent children. Too many new businesses quickly contribute to a high bankruptcy rate. If we are ever to understand the predictable variations in the outcomes of charter schools, a longitudinal ethnographic methodology will be required (see, for example, Muncey and McQuillan, 1996).

I am not suggesting that we could or should study these questions in regard to all charter schools. Nor do I wish to convey the impression that restricting such studies to a sample of these schools will be easy or inexpensive. But if in regard to educational problems and policy we seek to avoid the worst features of the quick-fix, flying-blind stance, these questions cannot be ignored. Political leaders know this in regard to problems of health such as AIDS and cancer, which is why we have the Federal Drug Administration, the Center for Disease Control, and the National Institutes of Health. Unfortunately, the same cannot be said for state departments of education or the federal Department of Education. When President Clinton announced that he would seek funding for three thousand additional charter schools, neither he nor the Secretary of Education said anything to suggest that in regard to this new initiative they were unimprisoning themselves from a self-defeating repetition compulsion that has been the hallmark of educational reformers.

I trust that this addendum does not obscure the fact that I regard charter schools as a long-overdue recognition that our educational system and its governance are incapable of reforming themselves. Despite this, and because of my experience and advanced age, I am unable to wax enthusiastic about the quality of what we will learn. If I am old, so is the story. It is like the point of my favorite Jewish joke, the one about the journalist assigned to the Jerusalem bureau of his newspaper. He gets an apartment overlooking the Wailing Wall. After several weeks he becomes aware that regardless of when he looks at the Wall, he sees this old Jew praying vigorously. There may be, he decides, a story here. He goes down, introduces himself, and asks what the old Jew is praying for every day at the Wall. "What am I praying for? First I pray for world peace. Then I pray for the brotherhood of man. I go home, have a cup of tea, and come back and pray for the eradication of illness and disease from the earth." The journalist is taken with the old Jew's passion, sincerity, and persistence. "You mean you come every day to the Wall to pray for these things?" The old Jew nods. The journalist is astonished. "How long have you been coming to the Wall to pray for these wonderful things?" The old Jew becomes reflective and then says, "How long? Maybe twenty, twenty-five years." The journalist is flabbergasted. "You mean to say that you have been coming all these years to the Wall to pray for these things?" The old Jew nods. The journalist then asks, "How does it feel to come to the Wall all of those years to pray for these things?" To which the old Jew replies, "How does it feel? It feels like talking to a wall."

Chapter Eight

Our Expectations of Political Leaders

We are used to depending on the forecasts of meteorologists to tell us what weather conditions we might expect over the next three or four days. We know, because they have told us, that forecasts beyond a few days get increasingly unreliable. Yet meteorologists are encouraged and supported to seek more accurate forecasts for longer periods of time, not for the hell of it, so to speak, but because increased accuracy will prevent loss of life and property. Most weather disasters are of a kind that come with ferocity, confront us with an immediacy we pray we will be able to endure until our world takes on aspects of accustomed normality. But there is another kind of disaster that never "comes," we do not know it is "here," we do not label it until its implacable destructiveness becomes visually apparent. Drought is the clearest example; civilizations have disappeared or been damaged forever by droughts. Today we are witness to a raging scientific controversy about a possible "greenhouse effect": Has the ozone layer become dangerously thin, has our atmosphere heated up and, if it continues, will the levels of our oceans and the contours of our continents change? And what about the climatic consequences of the elimination of rain forests because of human thoughtlessness and ignorance? In these kinds of instances the fear of some people is that an irreversible change has occurred and we are not taking steps to contain it, or we are acting too late.

Social change, of which school change is but one aspect, is in the second category—that is, we become aware of a change only after that change has begun to be recognized and labeled. Social change is not an intended phenomenon; it is largely (not exclusively) an unintended, unpredicted phenomenon even though the initial cause of the social change is no great mystery. So, for example, the social change so much a feature of the past five decades is inexplicable apart from an understanding of how World War II started, was conducted, and ended (Sarason, 1996a). Indeed, that wars transform societies is an old truth; predicting the substance and form of those transformations is quite another matter. It is one thing to say that World War II guaranteed a mammoth postwar social change, regardless of which side won; it is another thing to claim that the social change was immediately apparent and not preceded by an interval in which the desire to return to normalcy made early recognition of the social change virtually impossible. What is fascinating about social change is that it becomes understandable retrospectively but that understanding (right or wrong) brings to the fore the prospective question: How will that discerned social change get played out?

In regard to school change the prospective question is very high on the list of social anxieties: What are the likely consequences of an educational system that cannot narrow the gap between the haves and the have-nots, and, in addition and in general, decreases rather than increases interest in and motivation for learning? *Unlike any other time in our national history, that prospective question has not been off the social agenda for the past half century.* A lot of other aspects of the social change have been on the social agenda during these decades but none has had the insistence and persistence of schooling and race.

In previous chapters I have stressed that in regard to schooling the prospective question has not been based on a satisfactory answer to the retrospective one: What contributed to the exposure of the inadequacies of our schools and the intractability of those inadequacies to reform? Absent any satisfactory answer to the retrospective question, the programs suggested by the prospective question will, I predict, contribute more evidence for intractability.

Some readers will be surprised to learn that there was a truly massive educational program, legislated near the end of World War II, that forever changed this society in ways that no one has ever seen fit to criticize. I refer to the GI Bill of Rights, of which millions of veterans took advantage. Let me sketch the background and purposes of that bill because of its possible significance for schooling below the college level.

The catastrophe called the Great Depression was still fresh in the minds of all adults, veterans or not. And there were a great many veterans; of a population of 150 million people, approximately 15 million served in the armed forces. The number of veterans incurring a physical or mental impairment was very high. Between the veterans and their friends and families, it is not an exaggeration to say that the lives of very few people escaped the negative impact of the war.

It was a long war. Plans and ambitions had to be put on hold. Careers were interrupted. Personal lives and outlooks changed in response to ever-present dangers, sexual deprivation, military life, and exposure to new cultures. An anxiety-arousing social question arose as the end of the war neared: Could the economy accommodate several million eager-to-be-released veterans, especially in the face of the fact that a substantial part of the war-oriented economy would no longer remain in production?

The long and short of it is that political leaders saw the immediate postwar years as perilous ones, containing the poisonous seeds of social upheaval and another economic depression. Side by side with these forebodings was the felt moral obligation of a grateful society to do whatever could and needed to be done to give veterans the opportunity to reshape their lives in whatever ways they saw fit. The crucial word in the title of the bill is "rights." Veterans had rights that a nation was obligated to respect; they were not a homogenized mass for whom officialdom would set a direction and make decisions. Here are some of the features of the bill:

- A veteran could enroll in any program in any accredited college, university, or vocational school, here or abroad.
- Tuition and fees were paid by the government.
- There was an allowance for books.
- There was a monthly subsistence allowance for the veteran, wife, child.
- Centers for personal and vocational counseling were available to veterans.

It is unfortunate and deplorable that the social sciences never saw fit to study the GI Bill in terms of how many lives were redirected, of careers changed, of alterations in the stability of the nuclear family, of changes in the culture and complexity of colleges and universities, and the like. Keep in mind that we are not talking about a few thousand or a few hundred thousand veterans but of somewhere between five and ten (or more) million veterans who sought to take advantage of the unprecedented opportunity to refashion their lives through education.

For my present purposes, the significances of the GI Bill are several. First, the political leadership knew that it was confronted with a prospective scenario that could dilute, if not negate, the fruits of victory in war. Second, that scenario was to a significant degree informed by the still vivid memories of the Great Depression—it was also informed by experience with World War I veterans, who responded to the Great Depression by demonstrating against what they regarded as a niggardly, ungrateful government. Third, and quite unusual, decision-making power as to how and where the veteran would exploit the legislation was the domain of the veteran, a power largely respected and supported by colleges and universities willing to be flexible and sensitive to returning veterans for whom the campus was the polar opposite of military installations. Fourth, having decided on a course of action that was basically preventive in orientation, the political leadership did not shrink from the financial costs of that course of action.

I am not trying to convey the impression that the GI Bill was an outgrowth of a linear, rational process in which uncertainty and fear were in the background, the outcomes clear and desirable, and the law of unintended consequences had been repealed. What I wish to emphasize is that there was a knowledge of and respect for a troubled economic past that had taken a war to submerge; the fear that that past would reappear; the specter of millions of veterans returning to a civilian life unprepared and unable to meet their needs and expectations; the dread of civil strife. It was a mix of attitudes, memories, fears that required bold action before the social scene would become marked by civil unrest. Political leaders acted more because they felt they had to act and less because they were convinced that the legislation would serve its intended purpose, let alone that it would alter lives and institutions in the most pervasive ways.

In regard to school change the situation is both similar and different. It is different in that there is little or no perceived sense of immediacy. The problem is seen as serious, but it has been around a long time, its threat to the social fabric real but not yet immediate; in the future as in the past the problem can be contained. Furthermore, we really do not know why our past efforts have been so without success.

It is similar in that we know that the inadequacies of our urban schools—related as they are to issues of race, ethnicity, and class—are year by year increasingly consigning students to jobs that do not exist or for which students are unprepared; they are catapulted into an electronic-computer-telecommunication world that has no place for them. In a very abstract way some political leaders know that when there is no place in the arena of work for a significant part of the population—the young part not noted for its passivity and lack of hopes and dreams—the odds that there will be trouble ahead markedly increase. It is a part of the population that has no voice, that does not convey its individual and group dynamics to the rest of society except as its attitudes and actions are read or heard as worrisome signals by the others. What these political leaders know in the abstract they cannot use as a basis for school change because the evidence is clear that their proposals have been tried in the past, with no discernible effect. In regard to the veterans of World War II political leaders did not have to ask questions about prewar policies and practices because the evidence was overwhelming, truly overwhelming, that the VA medical programs were qualitatively and quantitatively deficient, and there had been no educational program for veterans. In regard to school change political leaders know that the history of school reform is a thick and discouraging one in which it appears that what could be tried was tried—except that no one suggested that perhaps the traditional undergirding assumptions of our school systems should be radically altered. As I have indicated, the concept of the charter school is the first indication that political leaders, perhaps unbeknownst to themselves, are challenging the legitimacy of the system qua system. It is also (perhaps) an indication that the need for school change is taking on a degree of immediacy and compellingness it did not have before.

In his book *Maximum Feasible Misunderstanding,* Moynihan (1969) tells the story of how in light of the Job Corps program in the War on Poverty he thought it would be instructive to read about the Civilian Conservation Corps (CCC) in the New Deal of the 1930s. He found that the government contained no record, no description, no evaluation of the CCC program; the government had no basis for learning from past successes or failures. In that same book, Moynihan concentrates on the Community Action Program of Johnson's War on Poverty and concludes that the government did not know what it was doing; and what it was doing was legislating a transfer of power from the political system to indigenous community groups. As one who observed that transfer first-hand I can only criticize Moynihan for understatement. That does not mean that in principle I was opposed to that transfer but rather that there was no evidence whatsoever that such a transfer of power *in the way it was being proposed* stood a chance of achieving its stated purposes. Nor does it mean that you do nothing unless you have evidence to justify doing something. Darman (1996) has put it well: "The problem is not the visions. Americans across the political spectrum want to improve education, reduce violence, eliminate substance abuse, strengthen families, restore traditional values and increase opportunity for achieving the Dream. The problem is that we know little more now than we did in the 1960s about how, on a large scale, to achieve these shared objectives. And the reason is a continuing surrender to ignorance. Major public-policy initiatives are routinely advanced, but rarely do we organize to evaluate what works. We thus allow politicians to mislead us. Then we act like helpless victims." Darman is no left-winger or liberal, nor (to use his own words) a "pointy headed" academic. But neither is he a conservative ideologue who would take pleasure from a government that disconnected its telephone service and went away for a long sabbatical. Whatever he is, he has put his finger on the theme of this book: we have a right to expect that politicians in high office will feel obliged to become so knowledgeable about the important problems besetting the society that they will refrain from taking a blunderbuss stance where the target has not been identified and there is no way one can learn from failure. In addition, in a relatively small number of instances, they will support—fiscally and timewise—the implementation of a reform in real-life conditions and with built-in means to pinpoint errors of omission and commission that will be corrected and tested in a subsequent, more sophisticated demonstration. As with other parts of government (for example, the Food and Drug Administration, Department of Agriculture, National Institutes of Health) no new solution will be encouraged or supported without prior credible evidence that most of its intended purposes can be achieved.

Good intentions are not enough. Personal anecdote and opinion are not to be sneezed at, but certainly they should not be confused with evidence. Fashionable terms or labels like "high standards," "charter schools," "vouchers," "privatization," "site-based management"—or anything that suggests technology as a universal solvent of educational problems—may sound innovative and attractive but, in Darman's words, you do not bet the system on a hunch or feeling. Hunch and feeling do play a role in new learning but one should never assume ahead of time that these inner promptings should be treated other than with respectful skepticism.

In regard to educational reform I agree with Darman's assertion that politicians have misled the general public (and misspent its money). I would go so far as to say that these politicians had little interest in, and therefore gave little attention to, the substance and history of the post–World War II educational reform movement. I say that because our more recent presidents have never given the slightest indication that they made it their business to become knowledgeable about the problem—they deserve the description "deep down, he is shallow." About a problem they say is crucial for societal traditions and welfare, a problem they say has defeated us in the past, a problem they say is deserving of our moral and fiscal support—having said this and more the fact remains that their articulated concerns mask a pervasive ignorance. They do not mislead us in direction—that is excusable—but in conveying the impression that they know what they are talking about. In regard to educational reform they do not know what they are talking about, and on those rare occasions when they say something that suggests they are getting near the heart of the problem (for example, the significance of charter schools), it soon becomes obvious that they feel no obligation to test their proposals in the real world in a limited number of places. They are not able to distinguish between an assumption and a demonstrated fact.

Earlier in this book I asked this question: "When your child is graduated from high school, what is the one characteristic you hope your child has?" In regard to political leadership and educational reform I would put the question this way: "When a president leaves office, what is the one characteristic you would want that president to have demonstrated?" My answer is that the president (or others in high office) should have demonstrated a willingness to learn, a modesty that acknowledges that the more you learn, the more you have and want to learn, and the courage to share personal experience of change and complexity with a public for whom the words *courage* and *leadership*, when juxtaposed, form an oxymoron. When it comes to school change, we should cease regarding our political leaders as exempt from criticism, as if there are more important things for them to think about. There are no more important things. What happens to our schools (especially urban ones) over the next two decades will be fateful for this country. To proceed as if that prediction is an indulgence in hyperbole, that somehow or other we will muddle through, is to take stances that produced the educational problem in the first place.

Nothing I have said in previous pages was meant to suggest that those elected to high political office should seek to gain more power to implement programs of school change. The further the seats of power from the sites that are the objects of change, the more likely the spirit and letter of change will be violated. That assertion may not deserve the status of a law but it does rest on a lot of experience with a lot of people in different times and places.

The power to educate, stimulate, and legislate is not synonymous with the power to influence, if by influence you mean that people are disposed to seriously consider what such leaders think and propose. To be influential does not require the exercise of formal power; it is the difference between making people feel that they must do something and that they want to do something, between their going along with you because they fear the consequences of not going along and because they choose to do so. In terms of consequences neither power nor influence is inherently superior to the other; when one resorts to one or the other (or some combination of both) depends on time, place, and experience. History is replete with leaders who had a great deal of formal power that they exercised in ways that limited their influence, just as there have been people whose influence was great but did not depend on formal power.

What I have done in previous pages is to criticize leaders more for errors of omission than for those of commission because the demonstrable inadequacies of what they sought to require others to do were in large measure the consequence of a failure to become knowledgeable about the failures of past leaders; to formulate that knowledge in clear ways; and to impart that new vision to people generally—that is, to give currency to ideas that need to be pondered, digested, and examined for utility.

If leaders are elected because a majority of the people agree with what those leaders say they will do, it is also the case that we expect them to bring to people's attention ideas, issues, problems that will at some point have untoward societal consequences if not put into currency. After all, we do not call people leaders because they are riveted on the present, ignorant of the past, and aware of the future only as extending to next month or perhaps to next year. We do not elect leaders only for them to act because they want to be perceived as responsive activists. We want a vision, some kind of map to the future, a proposal for a journey that most of us cannot conjure up if only because we are not paid to think about such things. But that is precisely what we pay those in high office to do: to use all resources of their office to track a present that has a past and a future. That is what they tend to do in regard to many problems, with a few notable exceptions of which education is in an ultimate sense the most fateful. In regard to education it has been all sound, no fury, no bangs, all whimpers, an audiocassette that endlessly repeats itself.

My criticism of political leaders is not a form of *argumentum ad hominem.* I do not impugn their motives, their personalities, or their intelligence. What I criticize is their failure to gain some understanding about why the consequences of the reform movement have been so discouraging and, no less important, their inability to entertain the possibility that the educational system as we know it is unrescuable in the sense that if we continue to do what we have done, the society will undergo transformations far more destabilizing than in the present or past. *When over a period of time a condition has been intractable to efforts to improve it, it is a sure-fire sign that something is radically wrong with the assumptions on which our actions are based.*

My conclusion about the unrescuability of the system was one I initially had difficulty accepting. But as years went by my resistance crumbled in the face of all my experience in schools. What finally convinced me was the recognition that no one—not teachers, not administrators, not researchers, not politicians or policymakers, and certainly not students—willed the present state of affairs. They were all caught up in a system that had no self-correcting features, a system utterly unable to create and sustain contexts of productive learning, indeed, a system in which the differences between these contexts of learning were hardly (if at all) discussed. The icing on this cake of vexation was provided by my meetings with policymakers and politicians in Washington and elsewhere. I realized that, however sincere their intentions, they knew nothing about schools and why the school culture, honed over many decades, would resist and defeat reforms attempting to alter the status quo. There are no villains. There is a system. You can see and touch villains, you cannot see a system. You have to conceptualize a system and you do that on two very different occasions: when you are essentially creating a system and when an existing system is faulty and you want to understand why. On both occasions the purposes of the system is the governing consideration. The fact is that most people—and in the case of political leaders it is all of them—think of education not as a system but in terms of its parts—teachers, administrators, local boards of education, colleges and universities, parents, state boards of education, and the legislative and executive branches of local, state, and national government. Clearly, there are many parts each of which is and sees itself as a stakeholder in the system. Equally clearly, precisely because no one is satisfied with educational outcomes, one would expect that reform efforts would be based on answers to two questions. In actual practice how do these parts relate to each other? Among those parts how much agreement is there about the purposes of the educational system? These questions have hardly been formulated, addressed, or studied. As a result the reform movement has been about parts, not about the system, not about how the purposes of parts are at cross-purposes to each other, not about how the concept of purpose loses both meaning and force in a system that is amazingly uncoordinated and that has more adversarial than cooperative features. It is no wonder that people within the system as well as an increasing fraction of the general public privately conclude that nothing will change. It is obvious why no one has ever said to me that if they were to start from scratch to create an educational system, they would come up with what we now have. They could not say what they could come up with because they had never thought of schools as being embedded in a very complicated system. And, I should add, when I pressed them to identify the parts of the existing system, it was surprising how many parts they left out.

What I have said here, as well as in earlier chapters, can be concretized by reference to *The Politics of Education* by John Brademas (1987). For two decades in the House of Representatives, Brademas played a major, often the crucial, role in the passage of education-related legislation. Perhaps more than any member of Congress, Brademas understood that improving the quality of schooling was no less than protecting the future of the country. His book deserves serious reading if only for its description of the obstacles the legislation encountered, the compromises negotiated, and how political leaders were defining problems. Several things are crystal clear in this book.

• *No one thought in terms of an educational system but rather in terms of discrete problems or discrete parts of the existing system.* It is not unfair to say that the cascade of legislation was a cascade of Band-Aids. There are times when Band-Aids are useful and effective—but only if the condition is not a systemic one. When the condition is systemic (and you do not know it), Band-Aids are at best useless and at worst harmful if they prevent you from examining the system.

• *Basic to the thinking of legislators was the assumption that what schools lacked were the resources to deal with the problems confronting them.* That is to say, there was nothing *basically* wrong or self-defeating about schools that an influx of money, materials, and personnel would not remedy. Put in another way, all the problems and inadequacies of schools *as they were* were in no way a reflection of how schools were organized and administered, of a narrow, stultifying conception of classroom learning, of a school culture in which collegiality and self-examination were absent. It is worth repeating: the legislation rested on the belief that money was the universal solvent that would permit schools to do more good for more students. One could say, to be charitable, that it was hoped that not only would schools do more for more students but they would do better for all students than they had been previously—that is, schools would transform themselves. It was a hope that ignored the realities.[1]

• *Rhetoric aside, presidents spend little time with matters educational, a reflection of the degree of their interest, curiosity, and sense of responsibility.* That was not true for President Lyndon Johnson who, like Brademas, was passionate about education but who had no understanding of what the problems were and whose tendency to act quickly short-circuited thinking.

At one point in his book Brademas says:

> Support from the national government has been crucial in enhancing our understanding of ourselves and our universe through, among other entities, the National Science Foundation, the National Institutes of Health, and the National Institute of Education. I felt a special commitment to the last initiative. When I introduced the bill to create the National Institute of Education, substantial percentages of the annual federal budgets for defense, agriculture, and health were earmarked for research and development. Yet when it came to education, which has such an enormous impact on our society, *the nation was not spending the small amount needed to generate thoughtful, objective, analytical evidence concerning how people teach and learn* [p. 13; italics added].

The italicized sentence is especially revealing of the view that teaching and learning—what takes place between teachers and students in classrooms—can be understood apart from the features of the system near and far—that is, apart from the culture of the school, from the local school system, and from other parts of the larger system. Teaching is inevitably an interpersonal affair but it also inevitably has the imprimatur of that larger system. I certainly

---

1. The one exception to those criticisms concerns Public Law 94-142, the 1975 Education for All Handicapped Children's Act, which in the most explicit way said that the schools could no longer treat handicapped children and their parents as they historically had. That act required that schools take the *individuality* of these students seriously, a respect for individuality not then or now accorded nonhandicapped students. Brademas fought successfully for that legislation, although he fails to see the relevance of that requirement for all students.

am not opposed to research on how teachers teach and students learn—but from my personal experience and reading the research literature, we know a good deal about these issues already. What we know should compel us to ask *why* teachers teach as they do, why classrooms are contexts for unproductive learning. The why question takes us beyond the encapsulated school and requires that we seek to understand how the system sustains and reinforces unproductive contexts both for teachers and students. As I have said countless times in my writings, teachers cannot create and sustain contexts of productive learning for students if those contexts do not exist for teachers. Those contexts do not exist for teachers now, and that is in large measure a consequence of the nature of the system. If Brademas makes anything crystal clear, it is that he came to have a very sophisticated understanding of how Congress works and why the actions, successful or not, of any individual congressman is totally inexplicable apart from the system of governance in which the individual operates. In his role as congressman he thought in system terms, which is why he came to be as respected as he was, as successful as he usually was in the passage of legislation. But when he thought about educational problems, he could not think in system terms, he accepted the system as it was, he dealt with parts. He could not transfer what he learned in the political system to the educational system.

Again, am I being unfair to political leaders? Am I expecting them to be more knowledgeable than they can or should be? I believe I am not. I expect them, no less than I do any other person, to face up to the fact that when efforts to improve a serious condition have generally failed one has to seek answers in the nature of the system in which the conditions arise. Yes, I expect political leaders to have that kind of wisdom, a kind of street smarts that at least some political leaders do acquire and apply in their political bailiwick.

Chapter Nine

Race: What the Constitutional Convention Bypassed

Beginning with World War II, political leaders have had to confront the morality and the social divisiveness associated with race and ethnicity. Those issues go back a long way in our national history; they were always in the social picture, occasionally giving rise to political compromises. The immediate cause of the Civil War was *not* slavery but the question of the rights of states to secede from the union—that is, it was a constitutional issue. Lincoln's place in history rests on his direct confrontation of that issue and then his issuance of the Emancipation Proclamation after the war had already taken a mammoth toll in human lives. For many decades after his assassination, no president directly, explicitly, and in a sustained way confronted the denial of civil rights to blacks.

It was an unintended consequence of World War II that it set the stage for the civil rights issue to begin to approach the social center stage. How can you justify total war against a Hitlerite fascism that was so morally sinful in regard to religion and race, and at the same time be irresolute about the denial of civil and human rights to segments of the American people? That irony did not go unnoticed or unexpressed in the black community and elsewhere. Doris Kearns Goodwin (1994) has described well and in detail why and how President Franklin Roosevelt was pressured to begin to take some initial steps not only to remedy the situation in the armed forces but to begin to recognize that the racial issue could no longer be kept in the social and political background. President Truman was the first national leader after Lincoln to deal forthrightly with the consequences of racial prejudice and the denial of civil rights.

Only once had the civil rights issue around race become associated with education and that was when toward the end of the nineteenth century the Supreme Court rendered the decision that "separate but equal" schools were constitutionally warranted. The unanimous 1954 desegregation decision of the Supreme Court changed all that and more, but not with the consequences most people (or the Court) expected. Few people expected that more than three decades later our urban schools would be more segregated than in 1954 and that some black educators would advocate for all-black schools. Those people, black and white, who breathed sighs of welcome relief for the decision envisioned a future in which blacks would receive an education that would enable many of them to lead more productive lives. What went unnoticed by these people is that the decision came at a time of mounting criticism of schools *as they then were*—that is, before the decision. Those criticisms came largely, not exclusively, from the academic community. Indeed, in the decade of the fifties a "great debate" about schooling developed between these critics and representatives of the educational community.[1] The Council for Basic Education was organized in 1956. Here is a summary of its program:

- Basic intellectual instruction must be the keystone of public education. The "hard" liberal curriculum, emphasizing English, mathematics, science, history, and foreign languages, must replace the purposeless "life adjustment" curriculum for all students, excluding those with clearly limited intelligence.
- Students with high ability must be provided with greater opportunities to develop to their maximum capacities.
- Standards must be developed to measure student achievement and to determine promotion to higher grades and classes.

---

1.   For a thoughtful discussion of that debate, see the educational sections of the now-defunct magazine *Saturday Review,* which covered the issue for a wide and educated audience during the 1950s and early 1960s under the editorship of Paul Woodring. Griswold (1959) and Bruner (1961a) are particularly worthwhile. In addition, Hanson (1959), Kelley (1947), Miller (1959), Rickover (1959, 1960), Skaife (1958), Bruner (1961b), and Koerner (1959) provide useful background.

- Teachers must be more adequately educated in the specialized subjects that they teach.
- When vocational training is offered, it must be duly subordinated to the primary function of the school: the development of intellectual discipline.
- Those school administrators who resist pressures to include programs in the curriculum more properly belonging to the home or church must be supported.

No one was more at the center of the debate than Admiral Rickover, whose critique of American education was very widely read. Here is a summary of the weaknesses he indicted:

- The preparation of teachers in this country was notoriously inadequate as compared with programs for European teachers that provided liberal education for its teachers equal to that of our lawyers and other professionals.
- Comprehensive multipurpose high schools with a variety of curricula from precollege preparation to vocational training impaired the development of the talented.
- Talented youth were not being identified and, therefore, few adequate provisions were made for them in the schools.
- Although Dewey improved what was once too autocratic a relationship between teacher and child, he did great harm to our traditional curriculum through his great influence in establishing the "Progressive Education" movement.
- There was a lack of national standards for children as well as for teachers. Local control impeded progress in education. "Everywhere in Europe there are uniform standards for educational goals, while the running and financing of schools is generally left to local initiative" (Rickover, 1960, p. 5).
- The business of allowing children to choose elective subjects to be studied in high school was disturbing, because it permitted them to decide on programs that could negatively affect their futures.

Need I point out that in the current debate today the utterances of political leaders (and others) betray an utter ignorance of how what they say and propose is identical to that said and proposed decades earlier, thereby allowing them to avoid the obligation of explaining why those earlier critiques and proposals either went nowhere or failed (as in the case of curriculum reform)?

I greeted the Court's decision with relief and dismay. Let me explain the dismay. For several years before the decision my research brought me into a number of schools and scores of classrooms. In addition, during that same period I collaborated with Burton Blatt of Southern Connecticut State College (now university) in the preparation of teachers, which widened and deepened my knowledge of and experience with teachers, especially in urban schools. What was disturbing to me in those experiences was the inescapable conclusion that the modal classroom lacked all the features of a context for productive learning for students and teachers. That is not to say that I predicted in the 1950s the decline in educational outcomes that was soon to begin. But after the Court's decision I had to predict that integrating schools would be no boon to blacks. Far from being a boon, my understanding of the culture of schools forced me to anticipate that integration would be divisive (to say the least) and fail of its purposes. And that opinion rested on, among other things, three words in the Court's decision: integration should proceed with "all deliberate speed."

Supreme Court justices are not educators and we do not expect them to be knowledgeable about learning, classrooms, and schools. Nevertheless, the words "all deliberate speed" implied that the solution was a logistical-engineering one—and that is precisely how political leaders interpreted and acted on the decision and those words. There is an irony here. When he was president of Columbia University, President Eisenhower had created a manpower research program in part because in World War II a large number of people had been rejected for military service because they were illiterate or considered mentally retarded; and a sizeable number of recruits who had been inducted turned out to be illiterate, presenting serious problems to the military. This had been described in detail in *The Uneducated,* a book that came out under the auspices of that research program (Ginzberg and Bray, 1953). One has to assume that President Eisenhower was aware of the contents of that book and, therefore, at some level knew that schools had failed to educate many people well before the Court's decision. The fact is that he resented the decision because of his prejudice in regard to blacks, as well as his opposition to an intrusive federal role (Ambrose, 1990). The irony is that although he probably knew well that American schools were far from achieving their stated purposes, he contributed nothing to the ongoing debate about schools, a debate that was unusually salient not only for blacks but for whites as well. The Supreme Court's decision was intended to improve the education of black students—that is, to enable them to receive the "quality" education of whites. But no one in the public arena, least of all the president, asked why, in light of the inadequacies of all or most predominantly white schools, one should expect blacks to flourish, especially in our urban schools.

It is beyond my purposes to go into the many factors that made integration a practical impossibility. Many readers lived through those years, and even those who did not know the several foci that surrounded the racial issue because those foci are still with us. Of those foci the power struggles are most relevant to my purposes; more specifically, the power conflicts of whites versus blacks, teachers versus parents, unions versus administrators and boards of education. To whom are schools responsible and who should therefore have a decisive role in matters of educational policy and decisions? In one way or another that question captures the heart of the matter because the different actors were never in doubt that the status quo was being challenged as never before. A clear example is one that on the surface said nothing about race. I refer to the 1975 federal legislation, Public Law 94-142, which was intended to prohibit or to drastically decrease the segregation of handicapped children in special classes, to require schools to employ the criterion of the "least restrictive alternative" in the placement decisions affecting handicapped students, and to require that parents participate in and approve any decision affecting their children. One of the people who helped draft that legislation told me that the group wanted, once and for all, to make it illegal for schools to continue to segregate handicapped children, to affect the lives of children without parental participation and approval. The drafters knew how schools would react to such a restriction on their accustomed ways, so they put in an appeals process allowing parents who felt their children were not receiving fair and appropriate treatment to go to higher state authorities and ultimately to the courts.

In its legal and moral basis, Public Law 94-142 is a direct descendant of the Supreme Court's desegregation decision. When that decision was handed down, diverse organizations advocating for children with handicapping conditions quickly saw it as a basis for lobbying state legislatures to enact laws that would make what they saw as a grossly insensitive educational community more responsive to the needs of these children. Several states did enact such legislation, which was influential in the passage of the federal legislation.

A very important feature of the history of that legislation was the role of evidence that segregated special classes, especially in urban areas, contained a very disproportionate number of minority students, mostly black, a fact that contributed fuel to the fires of controversy between schools and the black community in regard to school reform (Markowitz and Rosner, 1996). If Public Law 94-142 said nothing about race, race was in the background and in relatively short order a recognizable part of the foreground. The language of legislation is relatively cut and dried, and someone for whom the legislation has no direct personal significance has no way of knowing the emotional force that legislation had for others for whom it was personally salient. In regard to PL 94-142 it is hard to overestimate the depths of anger and frustration the members of those organizations directed at schools. The interested (or skeptical) reader should consult the several volumes of testimony—each weighing several pounds—given to congressional committees.

In the turmoil of the power struggles between blacks on one hand and educators and political leaders on the other hand, the advocates (black *and* white) for change took it as axiomatic that if power relationships changed—giving blacks more of a role in, or control of, educational policy and decision making—black and minority children would learn more. Why that would be so never got explained, and by that I mean that it is not self-evident that altering power relationships, or the skin color of teachers and administrators, or the curriculum, or all of these, will change the regularities characteristic of the learning context in the modal classroom. All these changes may be necessary but they are not sufficient to transform a context of unproductive learning into a productive one. That kind of transformation requires a changed pedagogy derived from a very different conception of the learning process and its context. None of these considerations got raised or discussed. No one asked why long before the 1954 desegregation decision many knowledgeable observers (for example, Aiken, 1942) were devastatingly critical of schools that were all white. In his presidential address to the American Psychological Society in 1899, John Dewey voiced criticisms of schools that differ little from later criticisms by others, and there are those who say his analyses and descriptions are unfortunately and remarkably cogent today.

Blacks saw and still see the problem in terms of power. So do our ahistorical political leaders. As a consequence, the nature and context of productive learning go undiscussed, as if that kind of learning is not what schooling is about, regardless of the color and ethnicity of the learners. In the social arena a lot of things that should be discussed are not going to be discussed—until a gathering social storm sets the stage for the possibility that a crucial undiscussed issue will come to the fore.

In regard to the racial issue, the portents of a gathering storm are hard to ignore, portents well adumbrated by Myrdal in his 1944 book *An American Dilemma*. That book was written before the social upheavals and changes brought about by World War II (Sarason, 1996a). One of those changes involved a dramatically altered relationship between education and employment, a relationship of crucial importance to blacks in an era of technological transformations that require diverse kinds of literacy if one is to have or climb anything resembling a career ladder. That is not news to the black leadership or to the political and business establishments; they are all quite aware of the percolating, destabilizing consequences of the situation, especially in our cities. They know that the situation is a dynamic one: it is not improving, it feeds upon itself, it is a festering sore for which past and present Band-Aids will be as effective as commanding the ocean waves to cease. Matters have not been helped, of course, by those who believe that blacks are on average genetically inferior and that their cultural-familial attitudes and practices are inimical to and undervalue education. The genetic argument is a classic example of the one-simple-answer fallacy, in this case yielding an answer that is both scientifically premature and wrong. The cultural argument confuses cause and effect and ignores history in two respects. First, it ignores the fact that every immigrant group that came to this country was for decades viewed as intellectually inferior and a threat to the societal fabric. Second, it glosses over the fact that blacks were not immigrants. They came as slaves, they were treated as slaves, not over decades but over a couple of centuries. Were it not for historians, black and white, we (whites who read history) could not comprehend the *psychological* consequences of slavery "socially inherited" and reinforced in generations of blacks since the Civil War. It is not playing fast and loose with the facts of social history to say that for all practical purposes Lincoln's Emancipation Proclamation was not taken seriously until World War II and its aftermath. As I have said elsewhere (Sarason, 1973), attitudes honed over the centuries will not soon change.

Why did I feel compelled to write the previous paragraphs? Because of how blacks have reacted to my position that their proposals for educational reform will be as generally ineffective as proposals by whites have been for schools that are all or predominately white, let alone those that are mixed in race. You can improve the physical conditions of schools, you can alter power relationships and introduce new curricula, you can employ computers in the classroom, give parents vouchers, start magnet schools, go the privatization route, start charter schools; you can employ black teachers only; you can ensure that black history will be taught; you can have all-black male or female schools, you can institute block programming; you can lengthen the school year— you can do all these things, each of which may contain a kernel of truth, but if you do not come to grips with what we know about productive learning, the outcomes you desire will be at best minimally met, and at worst not met at all. And if you take what we know seriously, you will see the need for other changes that will be difficult to achieve (Sarason, 1997).

If whites have viewed my position as irresponsibly radical or nihilistic, so have blacks, especially when I add that what I propose will take a long time for desirable outcomes to be generally evident—not in a school here and a school there, but generally. I am, of course, not opposed to demonstration schools. But demonstration schools that remain encapsulated demonstrations and do not spread are footnotes in the history of education. It used to be that many colleges and universities had their own experimental or lab schools. The classrooms of many of them reflected a deliberate attempt to be serious about the features of productive learning. One of the reasons most of them went out of existence was the realization that these schools were educational oases dramatically atypical compared with schools generally. What they demonstrated spread nowhere. They were small schools, they selected their students (and, therefore, their parents), they selected their teachers, they had ample support services, and they were stimulating places for would-be teachers. They were based on a theory of osmosis or contagion: somehow the fires of their accomplishments would spread beyond the campus. It doesn't and will not work that way. Illness spreads that way, but not health.

What happens in our cities will determine the fate of this country. Political leaders know that. They know that the economic health of cities is shaky indeed. And they know that those who do not live in the cities see them as personally unsafe places with high rates of crime. And political leaders read the statistics about the low achievement test scores of city children as well as about drugs and violence in those schools. And if they do not know, or cannot agree on, what to do, they do agree that schools have to change. In regard to the economic factor these leaders make their obligatory visit to slums and propose "empowerment zones" and other programs. They understand the direct and indirect fiscal consequences of unemployment and underemployment. But, in my opinion, they know next to nothing about schooling, which is to say they know nothing about productive learning. Back in the 1960s and 1970s there were occasions when I allowed myself to believe that some black leaders were beginning to see the issue, the basic issue. I heard what I wanted to hear but I heard wrong. There are those who see me as a self-appointed prophet of doom and gloom who would not recognize progress if it hit him in the face. I hope they are right, although I will be elsewhere when the results are tallied. In defense I can only say that my prophecies began in 1965—offered gingerly, semi-explicitly, and with some uncertainty—and they have so far, unfortunately, been confirmed.

I ask the reader to ponder two scenarios. The first is that it is the early 1960s and the educational reform movement is picking up steam, fueled by money, passion, theories, and programs for action. You were, like a lot of people, optimistic; change—discernible, desirable change—justified your prediction that these beginning steps would pay off, not in 1970 or even 1980 but certainly by the end of the millennium. What you hoped for clearly has not been achieved. Please explain. The second scenario places you in the year 2020. The desired outcomes of current reforms are not in evidence. What will your explanation be? There will be no simple explanation because the problem is such a complex one. There is no silver bullet, and in emphasizing the concept of productive learning I do not claim that status for it. What I do claim is that what we do know about that concept has not yet been taken seriously and, therefore, if other facets of the American dilemma are not informed by that concept, little or nothing should be expected from current reform efforts. As I indicated in my book *How Schools Might Be Governed and Why* (1997), productive learning is not a silver bullet but a key that will open a door. Only after we pass through that door will we discover where and why we were misled in the past—and the thorny problems with which we will have to deal in the future.

References

Aiken, W. A. *The Story of the Eight Year Study with Conclusions and Recommendations.* New York: HarperCollins, 1942.

Ambrose, S. E. *Eisenhower: Soldier and President.* New York: Simon & Schuster, 1990.

Arkes, H. "Jefferson on Race." *New Criterion,* 1997, *15*(5), 26–31.

Berman, P., and McLaughlin, W. *Federal Programs Supporting Educational Change,* Vol. 8: *Implementing and Sustaining Innovation.* Santa Monica, Calif.: Rand Corporation, 1978.

Bowman, J. "Ken Burns Does Jefferson." *New Criterion,* 1997, *15*(8), 53–58.

Brademas, J. *The Politics of Education.* Norman: University of Oklahoma Press, 1987.

Bruner, J. S. "After John Dewey, What?" *Saturday Review,* 1961a, *44,* 58–59.

Bruner, J. S. *The Process of Education.* Cambridge, Mass.: Harvard University Press, 1961b.

Cassidy, J. "The Decline of Economics." *New Yorker,* Dec. 2, 1996, pp. 60–64.

Cavanaugh, J. "Evolving Role for Police Officers in Schools." *New York Times,* Jan. 5, 1997, Connecticut section.

Clay, M. "Implementing Reading Recovery: Systemic Adaptations to an Educational Innovation." *New Zealand Journal of Educational Studies,* 1990, *22,* 35–58.

Commager, H. S. *Jefferson, Nationalism and the Enlightenment.* New York: Braziller, 1975.

Cowen, E. *School-Based Prevention for Children at Risk.* Washington, D.C.: American Psychological Association, 1996.

Cuban, L. *How Teachers Taught.* New York: Teachers College Press, 1984.

Darling-Hammond, L. "The Right to Learn and the Advancement of Teaching: Research, Policy, and Practice for Democratic Education." *Educational Researcher,* 1996, *25*(6), 5–17.

Darman, R. "Riverboat Gambling with Government." *New York Times Magazine,* Dec. 1, 1996, p. 115.

Du Bois, W.E.B. "The Freedom to Learn." In P. S. Foner (ed.), *W.E.B. Du Bois Speaks*. Vol. 2. New York: Pathfinder Press, 1970. (Originally published 1949.)

Flexner, A. *Medical Education in the United States and Canada. A Report to the Carnegie Foundation for the Advancement of Teaching.* Washington, D.C.: Carnegie Foundation for the Advancement of Teaching, 1960. (Originally published 1910.)

Ginzberg, E., and Bray, D. *The Uneducated.* New York: Columbia University Press, 1953.

Goodlad, J. *In Praise of Education.* San Francisco: Jossey-Bass, 1997.

Goodwin, D. K. *Franklin and Eleanor Roosevelt: The Home Front in World War II.* New York: Simon & Schuster, 1994.

Gore, A. *From Red Tape to Results: Creating a Government That Works Better and Costs Less.* Report of the National Performance Review. Washington, D.C.: Government Printing Office, 1993a.

Gore, A. *Transforming Organizational Structures.* Washington, D.C.: Government Printing Office, 1993b.

Griswold, A. W. "American Education's Greatest Need." *Saturday Review,* Mar. 14, 1959, pp. 15–17.

Hanson, E. H. "Viewpoints." *Education,* 1959, *79,* 326–327.

Hirsch, E. D. *Cultural Literacy: What Every American Needs to Know.* Boston: Houghton Mifflin, 1987.

Joint Commission on Mental Illness and Health. New York: Basic Books, 1961.

Kelley, E. C. *Education for What Is Real.* New York: HarperCollins, 1947.

Koerner, J. D. "Basic Education." *Education,* 1959, *79,* 72–74.

Markowitz, G., and Rosner, D. *Children, Race, and Power: Kenneth and Mamie Clark's Northside Center.* Charlottesville: University Press of Virginia, 1996.

Miller, R. I. "Admiral Rickover on American Education." *Journal of Teacher Education,* 1959, *10,* 352–357.

Mosle, S. "What Really Matters in Education." *New York Times Magazine,* Oct. 27, 1996, pp. 44–47.

Moynihan, D. P. *Maximum Feasible Misunderstanding.* New York: Free Press, 1969.

Muncey, D. E., and McQuillan, P. J. *Reform and Resistance in Schools and Classrooms.* New Haven, Conn.: Yale University Press, 1996.

Musante, F. "The Right Stuff About a School." *New York Times,* Oct. 20, 1996, Connecticut section.

Myrdal, G. *An American Dilemma: The Negro Problem and American Democracy.* New York: HarperCollins, 1944.

National Commission on Excellence in Education. *A Nation at Risk: The Imperative for Educational Reform, a Report to the Secretary of Education.* Washington, D.C.: U.S. Department of Education, 1983.

National Commission on Teaching and America's Future. *What Matters Most: Teaching for America's Future.* New York: Teachers College, Columbia University, 1996.

National Education Summit Policy Statement. Report from the National Education Summit, Palisades, N.Y., Mar. 26–27, 1996. (Available from Louis Gerstner, chief executive officer, IBM.)

O'Brien, C. C. *The Long Affair: Thomas Jefferson and the French Revolution, 1785–1800.* Chicago: University of Chicago Press, 1996.

Pinnell, G. S. "What Is Reading Recovery?" *Arizona Reading Journal,* 1992, *20*(2), 61–66.

Pinnell, G. S., and others. "Comparing Instructional Models for the Literacy Education of High-Risk First Graders." *Reading Research Quarterly,* 1994, *29*(1), 9–39.

Ravitch, D. "Adventures in Wonderland: A Scholar in Washington." *American Scholar,* Autumn 1995, pp. 497–516.

Rickover, H. G. *Education and Freedom.* New York: Dutton, 1959.

Rickover, H. G. "Education in the USSR and the U.S.A." *Graduate Comment* (Wayne State University), 1960, *3*(3), 2–6.

Sarason, S. B. *The Creation of Settings and the Future Societies.* San Francisco: Jossey-Bass, 1972.

Sarason, S. B. "Jewishness, Blackishness and the Nature-Nurture Controversy." *American Psychologist,* 1973, *28*(11), 962–971.

Sarason, S. B. *The Culture of the School and the Problem of Change.* (2nd ed.) Needham Heights, Mass.: Allyn & Bacon, 1982.

Sarason, S. B. *Schooling in America: Scapegoat and Salvation.* New York: Free Press, 1983.

Sarason, S. B. *The Predictable Failure of Educational Reform: Can We Change Course Before It's Too Late?* San Francisco: Jossey-Bass, 1990.

Sarason, S. B. *Letters to a Serious Education President.* Thousand Oaks, Calif.: Corwin Press, 1992.

Sarason, S. B. *The Case for Change: Rethinking the Preparation of Educators.* San Francisco: Jossey-Bass, 1993a.

Sarason, S. B. *You Are Thinking of Teaching? Opportunities, Problems, Realities.* San Francisco: Jossey-Bass, 1993b.

Sarason, S. B. *Caring and Compassion in Clinical Practice.* Northvale, N.J.: Aronson, 1995a.

Sarason, S. B. *Parental Involvement and the Political Principle: Why the Existing Governance Structure of Schools Should Be Abolished.* San Francisco: Jossey-Bass, 1995b.

Sarason, S. B. *Barometers of Change: Individual, Educational, and Social Transformation.* San Francisco: Jossey-Bass, 1996a.

Sarason, S. B. *Revisiting the Culture of the School and the Problem of Change.* New York: Teachers College Press, 1996b.

Sarason, S. B. *How Schools Might Be Governed and Why.* New York: Teachers College Press, 1997.

Sarason, S. B. *Revisiting the Creation of Settings and the Future Societies.* San Francisco: New Lexington Press, forthcoming.

Sarason, S. B., Davidson, K., and Blatt, B. *The Preparation of Teachers.* Cambridge, Mass.: Brookline Books, 1986.

Sarason, S. B., and Hill, K. T. "The Relation of Test Anxiety and Defensiveness to Test and School Performance over the Elementary School Years." *Monograph of the Society for Research in Child Development,* 1966, *31*(2), serial no. 104.

Sarason, S. B., Hill, K. T., and Zimbardo, P. "A Longitudinal Study of the Relation of Test Anxiety to Performance on Intelligence and Achievement Tests." *Monographs of the Society for Research in Child Development,* 1964, *29*(7), serial no. 98.

Sarason, S. B., and Lorentz, E. M. *Crossing Boundaries: Collaboration, Coordination, and Making the Most of Limited Resources.* San Francisco: Jossey-Bass, 1998.

Shanker, A. "The Real Solution." *New York Times,* Sept. 29, 1996, Review of the Week section.

Shanker, A. "Remembering Teachers." *New York Times,* Dec. 29, 1996, Review of the Week section.

Sizer, T. *Horace's Hope.* Boston: Houghton Mifflin, 1996.

Skaife, R. A. "Conflicts Can Be Solved." *Education,* 1958, *78,* 387–391.

Slavin, R., and others. "Success for All: A Summary of Research." *Journal of Education for Students Placed at Risk,* 1996, *1*(1), 41–76.

Sternberg, R. *Successful Intelligence: How Practical and Creative Intelligence Determine Success in Life.* New York: Simon & Schuster, 1996.

Strupp, H. "The Tripartite Model and the Consumer Reports." *American Psychologist,* 1996, *51*(10), 1017–1024.

Susskind, E. "Questioning and Curiosity in the Elementary School Classroom." Unpublished doctoral dissertation, Department of Psychology, Yale University, 1969.

Toch, T., and Daniel, M. "Schools That Work." *U.S. News and World Report,* Oct. 7, 1996, pp. 58–64.

Trickett, E. *Living an Idea: Empowerment and Evolution of an Alternative School.* Cambridge, Mass.: Brookline Books, 1991.

Weiss, A. R. *Going It Alone.* Boston: Institute for Responsive Education, Northeastern University, 1997.

Wilson, K. *Redesigning Education.* New York: Teachers College Press, 1996.